FALLING INTO PLACE

Falling into Place

An Intimate Geography of Home

CATHERINE REID

Beacon Press, Boston

Beacon Press
Boston, Massachusetts
www.beacon.org

Beacon Press books
are published under the auspices of
the Unitarian Universalist Association of Congregations.

17 16 15 14   8 7 6 5 4 3 2 1

The following works have been previously published: "Song Heart Rail,"
in the *Bellevue Literary Review*; "Deciphering Bird," in *Heartstone*;
"When a Fox Skull No Longer Points Home," in *Hunger Mountain*;
"Companions," "Rescue," "Water Rhythms," "Tides," and "Salamander
Crossing," in *Isotope: A Journal of Literary Nature and Science Writing*;
"Hitched, Massachusetts, 2004," as "Getting Hitched v. the Trashing of
Marriage," in *The Massachusetts Review*; "Ox Blink," in *Redivider*; and
"After a Sweet Singing Fall Down," in *The Georgia Review*.

Photo by Cordelia Stanwood used with permission
from Stanwood Wildlife Sanctuary.

This book is printed on acid-free paper that
meets the uncoated paper ANSI/NISO specifications
for permanence as revised in 1992.

Text design and composition by Kim Arney

Library of Congress Cataloging-in-Publication Data

Reid, Catherine.
Falling into place : an intimate geography of home / Catherine Reid.
pages cm
Includes bibliographical references.
ISBN 978-0-8070-0992-5 (cloth)
I. Title.
AC8.R375 2013
814'.6—dc23
2013023311

To the memory of my grandmother
H. Ruth Dwelley
(1904–2005)

and to Holly Iglesias

Oh, earth, you are too wonderful for anybody to realize you.
Do any human beings ever realize life while they live it—
every, every minute?

—FROM EMILY'S SOLILOQUY IN *OUR TOWN*,
BY THORNTON WILDER

Contents

Song Heart Rail

ICE UNFURLS FROM THE window in the steam of morning sun, and we move into the day with coffee, with dreams, with whatever scenes we can remember from the night. We've had this ritual since we first woke up together, a way to linger over the life we cohabit in sleep, though our very different imaginations mean we never fully share it. My dreams are fairly straightforward, a reliving of earlier dramas, while Holly's—cinematic and multilayered—are part of the reason I read little fiction these days. It would be tough to find action wilder than her subconscious produces.

I tell her how I moved between worlds when an owl called in my dream and was still calling as I awakened. A second owl answered from deeper in the pines, a pair of great horned owls, keeping track of each other. I could feel them in a night sharp with stars and bitter air and knew the nesting had begun, their eggs timed to open on a cold February day.

Holly laughs; she can't believe that owls incubate eggs under a blanket of snow. She is more amused, however, at my selective hearing, that a noise I care about might wake me while another will not. She makes her point

1

by updating me on her son, who is seaming together the pieces after an awful rift with his dad. I'm not sure why she is bringing this up now, and then I get it: She talked on the phone with him in the night, and I never even heard her rush from the bed to the kitchen. I hadn't caught that other sound that gladdens my life—the tenor of her voice when she talks to one of her kids, like the softening air of April in a house still locked in winter's chill.

I slept through it all until the hooting of that owl.

I understand the mechanics of hearing; I even know most of the vocabulary—the tiny ear bones of hammer, anvil, and stirrup that vibrate in response to a sound wave; the fluid-filled cochlea that registers those vibrations; the hairs that relay the messages along nerve cells to the brain. I understand how discerning we are, too; that the sounds we prefer are the ones our bodies know best, like our fondness for the iambic foot that beats our heart rhythms.

But not all sound enters through our ears, at least not in my understanding of the world. I can't explain how it happens, how some sounds catch us and others don't, but it's on my mind when I show up for the first meeting of the Wetland Birds Project, believing that, as a volunteer, I will simply head out to some designated site with binoculars and a bird guide, make a list of what I hear, and then go home for lunch. But it's not that simple. First I will have to pass a quiz. I will have to sit inside a small room with other would-be volunteers and identify birds solely by their songs. To prepare, we're each given a tape of fifty likely calls and told to come back in several weeks for the test.

At home, I pull on headphones and close my eyes. Almost immediately I'm back inside the wildlife refuge I frequented when living in North Florida, surrounded by the jostle and bicker of ducks and egrets in an orgy of feasting before the day's heat hardens the salt flats. Coots and moorhens whinny as they skitter in and out of the reeds. Herons and ibis clonk and grunt through the shallows, jabbing and shoving with a roughness they will repeat at dusk, when they fly into already crowded trees, hundreds of ungainly purple-black or white birds, elbowing a space in the dark crowns of oak and cypress.

I have to stop the tape. I had never thought about the ways the refuge and its noises might have crept into my own life. An upheaval in my days as a graduate student at Florida State, and I would head for the Gulf for the quiet of endless flat water. Yet in that land where oak and marsh meet pine islands and sea, even the fiddler crabs scrabble at high speed, and the alligator groans sound restless and haunting. All that resonance must have seeped into my cells. In a land teeming with the most primitive of needs—eat, sleep, mate, shove, shit, scratch, pule—the sounds had to have entered me, permeating skin and lungs, ratcheting joy into full-bodied exuberance, a tumbling taking place in the same weeks when Holly's and my paths first crossed, she, too, a new graduate student, she, too, attending Quaker Meeting, she, too, on the editorial board of a newly launched literary journal.

Here in western Massachusetts, where we moved several years later, everything is quieter, at least on the surface—the woods, the ponds, the fumbling, my heart. Most of the time, I like the familiarity of it; I like having to work to find the source of some noise. But sometimes the silence confuses me; I miss the bump of bodies, the thrash of wings and feet, the wrangling of high-volume Carolina wrens. Here, a great blue heron feeds by itself, and we nod at the shared solemnity. A raven calls from a rocky ridge, and we listen as though to a sage.

This tape recording, however, suggests that north-south distinctions can't tell the whole story, that the wetlands contain a world of sound that I haven't fully experienced. I rewind the tape and start again. This time I find myself in a mosquito-filled dawn, the kind of hours when few of us choose to visit such sites, yet my body responds with a hunger to see and smell such a place, to know what lifts from the cattails and stirs from the silt.

I open my eyes and see the cat pacing in front of me, her eyes focused on my ears. I hear Holly's laugh and realize I repeated the hooded merganser's call out loud, *awww, whaaa*, a drawn-out, guttural sound, conjuring a creature more reptilian than avian, something low-bellied and unable to get airborne. As I compare the list of names against the calls I just heard, I imagine the birds' cries drifting over people living close to them, sleepers exposed in the deepest hours of their dreams. I see how impulse might grip them later in a day, having nothing to do with their workplaces, their gene pools, their lists of chores to be done. I imagine artists and musicians, drifting toward swamps before dawn and finding new themes for their work in the way air is sucked and poured by these elusive, secretive birds.

A few days later, a friend comes to visit, puts on a new CD, and I hear such a process made real. Composer Lee Hyla has interwoven ivory-billed woodpecker and piano and baritone. The bird's hard cry is a percussive

surprise—like "the high false note of a clarinet," as Audubon once wrote—and the sound takes us to the southern
swamps and old-growth forests that the bird last inhab-
ited. While the bird is probably extinct, its voice never
again to be heard in the wild, for the moment, here it is,
in this room, a call provided to Hyla by the Smithsonian,
and maybe finding a place right now, inside each of us,
to come forth sometime later when we are least aware of
the reason.

Late-winter storms have left a foot of snow where I
should be seeing garden, and I pass my free time with
the headphones on, repeating voices I hadn't learned as
a kid. It's a competitive thing, wanting to do well on
the quiz, but mostly it's an odd experience, listening to
a call isolated from the bird itself, with no hint of habitat or season, no sense of whether I'm looking into the
crown of a tree, a tangle of marsh grass, or the scrub at
the edge of a meadow. It's simply a call and then a man's
voice, reciting the bird's name, as disconnected from its
source as listening to a heartbeat and not taking into
account breath and hair and skin.

I work to affix visual images that will help me remember each call—the wood duck's squeak like air through a
party favor, the king rail's click like a hammer on metal,
the Virginia rail's wheeze like a windup toy losing speed.
The method works and I pass the quiz, though a few
names won't surface as fast as I want, refusing to slip off
my tongue the way song recently surfaced for Holly, when
I shouted out of a bad dream, and she started humming
a lullaby before she was fully awake, the soothing tune
returning both of us to sleep. She had years of practice,

however, through the raising of two children, and I am
still figuring out the many levels at which we listen.

It's cold when I conduct the first survey, even though it's
already two hours past dawn. But the rain has stopped at
last, after nine days of powerful storms and an afternoon
of hail. In the stillness, every twig and blade of grass is
mirrored in quiet water. Across the small pond, two fat
ducklings paddle and spin, no parent duck in sight, while
three swallows dart above. A muskrat angles away from
me, its swath of ripples distorting every image, but little
else moves in this post-storm cool.

I arrange the gear I'll need to make the necessary field
notes—compass, thermometer, binoculars, clipboard—
check the time, and start the tape. Each of the eight
birds selected for this study depends on cattail marshes
like these for its survival, and such marshes are being
destroyed at unprecedented rates. For too long wetlands
seemed undesirable—boggy, malarial, unbuildable—and
it took years to understand their role as the catch ba-
sins of floods, storing and filtering pollutants before they
drain into rivers. The health of such aquifers can be assessed by the health of these birds, which function the
way canaries do for miners.

The findings to date have been rather bleak. The king
rail may have been driven out of the region; both the
American and least bitterns are considered endangered;
and the sedge wren is now the rarest of all the state's
nesting songbirds. Two recent river spills add to the rising concern. In one, a derailed train car sent six thousand gallons of latex solution pouring into the water. In
the other, sulfuric acid was flushed into one of the larger

tributaries, killing two tons of fish in the first two miles, the acid so powerful it melted flesh on contact.

No bird calls back to the tape during the time that I wait, and I pack up the gear and drive to my next site, assigned to me because my kayak is light enough to drag through the woods and easy enough to paddle through the shallows of this dark pond. A wood duck explodes from a nearby nesting box; a hooded merganser watches from another. I wish they were proof of a fine water source, but they're more rugged than the birds I'm after and less choosy about where they take up residence. The birds I want to see teeter in a far more narrow zone.

I stow the equipment, lower into the kayak, and paddle to the opposite shore. Once there, I back into the cattails, strap the tape recorder to the deck, and settle in to wait. For the next few minutes my whole focus is on sound. Eventually I begin listing birds on the data mapping form, separating their calls from the lap of waves against the hull, the chuck of a distant chipmunk, a truck laboring up a nearby hill. But when the grebe's eerie call rises from the tape, suddenly it's twenty years ago and I'm back in northern Vermont, hearing this same cry from a nearby river. I never knew for sure whether it was even a bird I was hearing, as nothing about that habitat—hardscrabble farmland on the edge of boreal forest—was quite right for something that sounded more at home in the company of wild monkeys.

But this was it—a tiny, pied-billed grebe, barely twelve inches long, emitting such a weird cry that it burrowed deep into my brain and stayed there, rooted, for over two decades, until the combination of cold morning wetlands and conifers dislodged it.

A pair of noisy Canada geese (CAGO) brings me back
and I list all I hear, using the standard four-letter codes:
RWBL (red-winged blackbird). TRSW (tree swallows).
GRHE (green-backed heron), its sharp-edged cry like
the clacking of swords.

Once again, however, I hear none of the targeted birds.

After spending so much time with these calls, I feel them
occupying space inside me, as though this very act of
close listening, a kind of cupping of my whole body, has
fixed them in my cells. I still don't know what brings
them into consciousness, however, or how a sound might
trigger awareness before we even know that we've heard
it. What I do know is that there have been times over the
years when I walked across a field and knew I had to veer
left or right, fast, and each time I did, I soon saw what I
was avoiding—usually a stream of wasps zipping in and
out of an underground nest—probably because my body
had picked up some almost inaudible hum.

Sometimes, however, the timing is scrambled, as with
my father's recent heart surgery. He had very little warning, maybe a week or so to prepare, and in one of those
days he had seen a truck hit a deer. He told me about it
the day before he left for the hospital, and that he had
seen the deer hobble into the woods near his house but
hadn't been able to do anything about it.

I forgot about it, of course. My father's chest was being sawn open, his strongest and most fragile muscle
lifted out—the one we all suspected would fail him at
this very age—and imagining him healthy again was all
I could do. Afterward, I wanted nothing more than to
sit by his bedside with my mother and Holly, with my

brothers and sisters, and watch him open his eyes, and listen to him breathe, and take pleasure from the warming of his skin. And then he could cough, and then stand, and then eat a small meal on his own.

The fourth morning, the worst clearly over, we were slower to leave the house for the hospital. My mother had made a special breakfast, a way to thank us for staying with her during Dad's absence, and then something insisted I go outside. "I won't be long," I said, taking their dog and heading for the woods. I chose a direction I never take, past the old apple trees, over a fence, and through a screen of small hemlocks. And then I saw it, as though I had been summoned, as though its moan had called me to this site: The injured deer was just ahead, trying to move, its hind legs broken, a sudden jerk carrying it a few yards forward. When it collapsed, it pulled in its forelegs, its eyes never leaving us, its ears in constant motion.

I grabbed the dog. I watched the heave of the deer's sides. I felt its labored breathing and the silence of the woods. And then I knew I should call one of my three brothers, two of whom have guns and could dispatch it fast. But any free time they had would be spent at the hospital. So I called the police instead and left the dog inside. When the officers arrived, I led them to the deer, turning away as the single shot was fired. Almost immediately a weight lifted from my shoulders. Whatever sounds the deer might have been making—the flutter of its nose and ears, the pumping of its breath—had relaxed their hold on my limbs. Whatever terror we had shared was gone as well.

Two weeks later, as I pole my kayak through a snarl of laurel bushes, an American bittern booms so close the sound seems to come from inside the boat. I feel the vibrations against my back and thighs and wonder if I accidentally hit the recorder's play button when stowing the gear. Then I see the bird ahead of me, about twice the size of a crow, and poised to do battle if I insist on paddling forward.

I do. Carefully. At such close range, the bird's voice is not at all like a mallet against a stake, the usual description given for its call (or, as Thoreau once portrayed it, as if the bird "had taken the job of extending all the fences up the river to keep the cows from straying"). It sounds more like a bang on the skin of a long drum. "*Oong-ka-choonk*," according to the ornithologist Roger Tory Peterson, though I think you have to feel the shift in tongue action to know it, the big *oong* both a gulp and a click, a sound probably only the !Kung or Xhosa people can instinctively make.

Fortunately, it doesn't follow through on its threat, though it flies alongside my boat, keeping me warned and cautious. As I back into the cattails, the bittern positions itself in a shrub barely three kayak-lengths away. I spread out my gear. Slowly. Nothing startling; nothing that might be misconstrued. I once heard about a man impaled by a great blue heron, several inches of bill going straight into the man's chest when he ventured too close to the rookery. And though I have never heard anything frightening about bitterns—their best trick, after all, is camouflage, a slow lift of bill when they sense danger, their vertical brown stripes a perfect match for the play of light on reeds—I don't want to take any chances.

I turn on the tape recorder and brace myself as the bird hunkers into a posture that lets it tilt forward, white shoulder feathers flaring with each call. This bird has no wish to hide. This is his turf, and I am not welcome. He takes a gulp (*oong*), throws his bill upward (*ka*), then sucks back the sound in a great compression of neck (*choonk*), the noise like someone about to retch. I manage to make the required notes—wind speed of 2 on the Beaufort scale, compass reading of 200 degrees south, a rose-breasted grosbeak in the tree to my left— while keeping my right shoulder hoisted at an awkward angle above the clipboard, my paddle poised just below my hand. I could raise it in an instant, should the bird come any closer.

It doesn't. It's all bluster and brilliant shapes, "the genius of the bog," according to Thoreau, a loud and angry presence through the whole playing of the tape. I head for the pond's farther end; I repeat the process; a marsh wren delights me and the bittern doesn't quit.

Later in the day, I find myself imitating the sound and absurd neck compression, and wonder how long this bird will dwell within me.

On Father's Day, my dad seems tender with everyone, though particularly so, I think, with Holly. My reserved, cautious father, talking at length with her about her poetry, her mediation work, her grown children in Miami. At various moments, he seems surprised by the fine flavor of the chicken he's just grilled, by a granddaughter's school project, by the fact that his six kids turned into six adults, who can do everything that he once did and

collectively far more. He has to sit, it's all so staggering. And then, when it comes time for Holly and me to
leave, he stands and reaches out to us. "Take care of each
other," he says, as he hugs each of us against his scarred
chest. His look as I close the car door says all I need to
hear. *It's a very good thing, the two of you together.*

On the drive home, I have a hard time keeping my
eyes dry enough to see the road. I don't know when the
transition happened, when he went from cool, distant
man to emotional, open-armed father. I wasn't around
to see how hard he must have struggled, after those awful couple of years when we didn't speak to each other. I
don't think I'll ever know how he reconciled the fact that
the choices of my life weren't necessarily a rejection of
his and that my love of women in no way subtracts from
my big love of him.

And because I didn't witness it, I'm free to imagine
an osmotic process, ideas emanating from the landscape and the people who inhabit it, new ways of being
with one another seeping into my father as he slept and
dreamed, as he worked through his days and listened to
his heart and watched his kids leave home, one by one.
I imagine possibility lodging in inner recesses the way a
sound does, and as likely to surface at sudden odd times.
The smell of a neck, the curve of a finger, the spike of a
cowlick that won't be denied, and it all comes tumbling
back, in no particular sequence—he's a new dad at the
hospital, cradling a baby in his arms; he's saying goodbye
to his mother, who died when he was much too young;
he's loving his wife and he's stunned once again that they
created so much together.

I paddle slowly across the pond to do the last survey of the season. Though just cresting the horizon, the sun is already hot on my skin and on the buds of the pond lilies, their petals peeling back in the strong light. The travel is trickier today than on my previous visits—the water level is lower, the floating plants denser—but I feel even more present in the place. Most of the season's recklessness is over, and the rush of birds to mate and nest has calmed. I take my time getting to the first site, as fingers of mist lift from the last of the night's shadows.

I miss the bittern, which doesn't respond to the taped *Oong-ka-choonk*. Either it has left the area or it's on a nest and can't risk drawing attention to itself or to its mate. I do hear a marsh wren, however, a bird a mere fraction of the bittern's size yet almost as loud, its reedy song like an organ grinder cranking much too fast.

Squinting and a ball cap help with some of the glare, as I paddle the pond's length and set up again. I will miss this ritual—checking time, temperature, and wind speed; arranging binoculars and pencil, clipboard and code sheet; listening for what's in the area before starting the tape. I will miss having such focus devoted to sound. But I won't mind sleeping another hour or two past dawn. Nor will I be sorry to spend more time with coffee and the telling of our dreams.

RWBL. TRSW.

Then, right next to me, a rail calls, a Virginia rail, talking back to the tape, and suddenly the boat feels too tight to contain all I'm feeling. The tape repeats the call and so does the bird, a few feet away inside a dense stand of cattails. And then it appears, so close I could touch it. It struts like a chicken, in and out of spaces that seem too narrow for its body, and I see how "thin as a rail"

comes from the way it compresses itself laterally. All the
while it clicks and wheezes, a hammer on an anvil, a bag-
pipe filling and emptying.

When it reaches the end of the kayak, it flies across the
narrow channel and continues calling and watching me.
And then two otters pop up ten feet away, all whiskers
and dark eyes. They tilt their heads, they whimper their
questions, they snort and disappear. Another rail calls;
another wren speeds into song. And then it's more din
than I have heard all spring—grosbeaks and waxwings
in the trees, grackles and blackbirds back and forth between stumps, swallows and more swallows flitting after
insects, along with turtle plonks, the croak of frogs, and
a crashing on land that sounds clumsy and large.

I don't want the tape or the morning to end. I don't
want the sun to rise higher or the mosquitoes to arrive
and trap me in the boat. But soon they do; the air starts
to hum, and I pack up my gear and return to the car.

A note under the wiper blade explains the last loud
noise in the woods, a message written by the woman
who gave me permission to cross her land. "Black bear
at south end of pond," it says. I wave at the nearby house
then slide the kayak onto the roof rack, my shirt sticking
to my back in the heat. As I strap it down, stowing the
paddle and gear inside, I know I've located all the evidence anyone needs—neighbors and rails and otters and
my father—to allay whatever concerns might still exist
about the health of this small valley.

Water Rhythms

WHEN WATER DOESN'T FLOW from a faucet; when a house isn't connected to city pipes; when every liquid ounce has to be driven in by truck or carried in gallon jugs; when we have to go to the source for every pail and sip—the well, the spring, the reservoir, the river—then we remember how we depend on it, how it fattens our food and veins and humors. We savor it. We dole it out.

We sense again its steady rhythm, which I hear in the voice of a friend when she describes her home by what she no longer has. "We used to live with a cistern," she says with some sadness. "We had to live our days around if and when there was water."

She says it as though reciting poetry, as though the experience contained many truths and each could be distilled into an image that succinct. But she and her partner do more than raise sheep and border collies; they also work regular jobs at other places and have to show up on time, whether or not water flows from the small reservoir.

"The catch," she says, "is that you can only live like that when everyone works on the land, the way the earlier farm families did. When you can set up a rhythm of

washing—clothes, bodies—that has everything to do with
available water and nothing to do with time of day. You
make sure there's enough for the animals; you make sure
everyone gets some to drink. You learn to shower when
you can and save dishwater if you have to, to throw on
the garden later in the day." But after many months of
trying to fit their lives into that cycle, they admitted they
needed a steadier flow and dug a deep well.

I know what she means, however; I lived the rhythm
as a child in those summer weeks that our family spent
at my grandfather's cabin in northern Vermont, where
all our drinking water came from a spring across the
small lake. We took turns paddling over, a chore none
of us minded—a quiet approach, a careful entry through
tall grass, a way of lowering the pail so that no silt was
stirred. And then a bucket of cool water to balance on
the way back—in the center of the canoe, up the uneven
steps of the bank, and into the kitchen without slopping
or dribbling. It was the drinking and teeth-brushing water, the cooking and tea-making water, the coffee and
lemonade and thirsty-in-the-night water. For everything
else—for everything that didn't come near our mouths—
we used what came from the lake. But the water that
we dippered, we loved for its taste and because we knew
where it rose up, secretive and splendid.

It was a rhythm I knew as an adult, too, the winters I
lived without plumbing and made do with rain buckets,
with ice or snow I melted in large trays on the woodstove. And it was a rhythm I felt in every cell in my body
for those four days I once fasted without food or water.
I had taken part in a demonstration, protesting a nuclear power plant being built on the banks of the Connecticut River, just upstream from where I had grown

up. I knew too well what "downriver" and "downwind" meant. I knew too well which railways would carry away radioactive wastes, which roads would turn into evacuation routes for families and school buses and emergency personnel. And I believed then and now that there is no acceptable way of storing toxic materials with century-long half-lives.

I was arrested and chose to fast, my tongue sticking to the roof of my mouth, my body feeling lighter and more brittle by the hour. Then, 2:00 a.m. on the fifth morning, they released me, a concerned guard offering me a glass of water on my way out. Afterward, almost rehydrated and on the back of a friend's motorcycle, everything in that moist night seemed connected by the sudden kindness of the guard and the water animating all of us—the deer in the headlight, my eyes tearing in the wind, the frogs' great leaps as they sponged across the road.

Tides

I THOUGHT I KNEW much about rivers, having grown up by the Green, which empties into the Deerfield and thence into the Connecticut. The Green was but a short run through the woods from our house, and as a child I found lots of reasons to be there: swimming, fishing, rafting, walking; a place to ice skate or hide out from school or keep clear of the troubles that often brewed at home. There I learned how curves are carved and banks shaped, the river chiseling new shortcuts during wild and littered springs. I watched floods fill the flatlands and ice bark the trees, and I followed fox and deer paths as they paralleled the feeder streams. I figured out how crayfish jerk backwards and raccoons wash and eat them, and I sat for hours in the evenings watching young beaver practice damming. Ducks and herons, minnows and backswimmers, paddling voles that I thought needed rescuing—I believed after all those years that I knew the habits of rivers. But living by the Deerfield makes me realize how much I have yet to learn.

On an early morning in town, I watch the play of light, the lift of mist, the drift of petals as they collect above the hydroelectric dam. Several swallows dart for insects. Someone pushes a stroller. Someone else aims a camera. The Bridge of Flowers in Shelburne Falls looks like a postcard. But I need a wilder and less traveled river, and I drive west and then north, where steep hills force the Deerfield through a narrow, rocky pass.

I park near Zoar Gap and wander the shore, around me a smell like that of clam flats, of things rotting and dead. The travel is tricky, a slick mud between me and the river, the low waters suggesting drier conditions than the last few weeks have been. But I'm too eager to be in the water to waste time contemplating mud. I wade out midstream, watching for that distinctive rise of a fish after an insect. The air is tender, the sun warm. I climb onto a large rock and look around, somewhat surprised that on this soft day I see no other people—no fishermen, no kayakers, no tubers. Mostly, though, the steady flow lulls me, the downward spill a reminder of all the constants in our lives—the pump of heart and lungs, the urge to eat and sleep, the need to love and be loved through the seasons and years.

And then, without realizing I made the decision, I push off from the rock and begin wading toward shore. The river has a new sound to it, something I probably heard but not consciously, something telling me to walk faster, to do so this minute. The ripples lap louder, and I pick up my pace; so do the bubbles that stream through the riffles. The current presses hard against my ankles and I have to place my feet with greater care. I aim for the light-colored rocks, which were dry just minutes before, avoiding all that's dark and algae-slick. I don't want to trip and bump downstream, with no way to get a purchase on slippery stones, and I don't know how much stronger this surge is going to run. I stumble; I can't get a foothold; I jar rocks loose in my scramble and have to use my hands to brace myself, until my feet gain a grip and I keep on. But so does the force, the noise, my splashing.

I reach the bank seconds before the water does, then it, too, is at the high tide mark, that line that looks crayon-drawn, inside it all the dirt and leaves and other debris left when the river last receded. I can't believe the change: The river is now twice as wide as when I arrived and flowing perhaps four times as hard. Now I understand what the signs describe, the ones placed at regular intervals wherever people might access the river, or those within earshot of the feeble alarm systems:

WARNING
RISING WATERS
Be constantly alert for a quick rise in the river
Water upstream may be released suddenly
at any time.

DANGER
Water rises after horn sounds
Please leave river

This is how that quick rise looks: Like a tide that just came up, with strength enough to level the thin-boned or unwary. The gates of an upstream dam opened, and the littoral zone was erased. This river—this waterway that looks and smells and sounds like a river—is not the kind I am used to. This is a manipulated energy field, with artificial highs and lows and regulated currents. Needs and tastes far from these steep hills and small communities can, in minutes, change a sleepy flat stream to churning whitewater. My world just shifted another few degrees, and I realize my earlier sense of rivers was more like time spent with a new lover, on vacation, in a world luscious and separate and untested. I have no idea what will happen after the alarm goes off, the coffee is drunk, and we return to the world of business and hard work.

Ox Blink

THE TRUCK LURCHES FROM side to side when Jack Roberts, a local logger, backs it up our driveway, and it shudders with each hoof step after he parks and leads out the first ox. When he reenters the truck and brings out the second one, everything around them—the barn, the studio, the big yellow truck—seems to shrink in size, the animals much taller than the six-foot-tall man.

I join them and feel thin, despite the thickness of my down coat, as we look over the remaining tall pines, our deal almost concluded. Our trees will become his lumber, sawn at his mill in town, a trade so close to even that no money will need to change hands. Both the barter and the oxen make the scene feel a century old, only none of these trees would have been part of the view, as all this land was pasture back then, bare hills all the way to the rivers.

It's too cold to stand for long, and Jack yokes the animals together with an ease that reveals his years of doing this. Each ox lost a mate this past year, the only partner either had ever known, and Jack is wary about how they will react to being together. A few weeks ago, he says, after he put them both in the same field, they went at each other so hard that one of their horns broke in the collision and blood spurted everywhere. The wound has healed, but the stunted horn remains, a reminder that they didn't choose to be bound together; this is Jack's idea.

The windchill is minus-twenty-something on this zero-degree day, and we expose little face and no hands. The oxen, however, seem animated by the cold, and Jack walks them down the hill and hooks their chain to a twenty-foot log from a pine tree he felled the previous day. They heave into the pulling, dragging it about fifty feet over frozen ground before he hollers for them to stop. Then they wait as he and I talk about trees and lumber prices and the animal he recently heard, crying like a baby behind his house in the night, an odd sound that someone told him later was a fisher, an animal we have barely begun to know as a neighbor.

Their big ox eyes close as he starts another story, about a calf killed a few years ago, in the next town to the north, the claw marks exactly like those of a mountain lion, which everyone knows were driven out of the region about a hundred years ago. And they stay closed as he describes a den that loggers have seen a few miles from here, occupied by animals that look more like wolves than coyotes, even though the last wolves were killed in the mid-1800s. But the weirdest change of all, he says, as puffs of steam escape the flutter of patient ox nostrils, has been the arrival of opossums. "I was collecting eggs in the henhouse one evening, and I almost slid my hand under one of them. It was all curled up on a nest, and I wasn't paying much attention in the dark, and I tell you, I came that close." He illustrates without taking off his gloves and shudders again at the proximity. "They sure are ugly fellows, aren't they?"

He gives his team the signal, and they toss their heads and snort and lean hard into the task, but Jack makes them stop again after another thirty feet. "They're too frisky," he says. He has to work them carefully at this point in the season so they don't abuse their legs, which right now support well over a ton of weight. In the summer, he says, they'll be even heavier, maybe three thousand pounds each, and all of it straining at the real test—to move several tons of concrete block at a county fair somewhere in New England, giving him the chance to add more blue ribbons to his collection.

With each hard gust of wind, the pines chatter and creak. An occasional branch breaks free, bouncing off other limbs on its way down, and I know I'll miss their sounds once the trees are gone—the fluttering noise of needles in a summer breeze and the crack and scrape of self-pruning limbs. The nakedness will be startling, but the field will be larger, our house will receive far more light, and the garden will finally get full sun all season.

At the top of the hill, Jack fits a peavey under the log and rolls it into the stack taking shape on the side yard. In the clearing, smells linger—hay and manure and pine and wood smoke—a steady presence against the sense of loss, which occurs each time a tree cracks from its sawn wedge and shudders down. That's when I most want to stand near tall beasts that feel like bulwarks against change; that's when I want to watch their sides move in and out with each breath, their eyelids lowering slowly with each blink. Time pauses until those long eyelashes lift, a space between one life and the next.

Jack says they have names—Bob and Mike—but he doesn't use them. He says, "This one is almost nine." "This one will be eleven on Father's Day." "This one I know better, the way you always get to know the one on the left side better."

He says, "It's hard to lose one after ten years. You get used to having them around." He turns away to hide his sadness, shouting the oxen back into action, and I head for the warm house, wondering if I'll feel the same way after losing these sturdy dark trees.

Unlike the pines on Holly's and my land—shabby and crowded and mostly double-boled, the result of pine weevils eating their tops years ago—the white pines in the Mohawk State Forest are straight and clean, some as much as 150 feet tall, like cathedral pillars holding high their green tops.

We gather near them to honor a friend who recently died, a forester who advocated for trees just like these, and, to celebrate his life, we're holding a tree-naming ceremony. On the way to the tree, soon to be known as Karl Davies, we pass through a field where the bones of a bear lie scattered by vultures and coyotes, black hairs and a large skull all that's left of its body. As we approach the Algonquin pines, the likes of which are hard to find anywhere else on this side of the continent, Bob Leverett, an expert on finding old growth forests, describes the Native American belief that the white pine is a sacred tree of peace. Out of respect for that association (his wife's lineage), he has given a few of these trees the names of people who worked for greater harmony among all living things.

We circle the tree chosen for Karl, and a few people speak, remembering him as an ally of forests, as an antiwar activist, and as a tall man who assessed woodlots with a tiny dog by his side. I catch sight of a brown creeper, inching up a nearby pine, its thin call like a distant voice in the wind, and I drift between it, the blue sky, and Susan, who stands closest to the tree, wrapped in her own quiet. She and Karl had met the previous year, before his cancer was diagnosed, which gave her little time to love him, but she did so when he was wracked and nauseous and morphine-stupid, and in those moments when he was radiant at being alive in her presence. Had he lived a few more days, they would have been married.

Lines from an E. E. Cummings poem come to me then, about "the leaping, greenly spirit of trees," and I imagine Karl's presence lingering in these woods, his greenly spirit joined with those of the trees. And yet, I also know about the risks involved in giving a human name to a tree. A freak lightning storm could blast the pine's core; a violent microburst could sheer its top tomorrow, and such disaster might affect our memories of all that came before, the way it did for my brother and his first wife, who planted a tree on an anniversary of their marriage. The tree died, they divorced, and Sally cried for a long time afterward. It had been an omen, she was sure.

On the way home, I pause near a favorite stand of hemlock, remembering the different things Karl and I noticed on those days when we wandered along the trails above this valley. It was with Karl that I became aware of how often I look toward the ground, hunting for stories in tracks or scat, fur or feathers; in contrast, Karl looked up, searching for stories far older than passing birds or animals or the evidence of ripe crops. The real histories are recorded higher up, he would point out, like global weather patterns, effects of pollution, and markers of lean or good times in crabbed or healthy growth. I arch back now and look for those signs but see mostly the paradox of hemlocks. The trees thrive in harsh places, often north-facing slopes, where the land is rocky and uneven, the light perpetually muted. Yet there is a tenderness about hemlocks, written all over their rough-plated length. Thick bark contrasts with delicate limbs, each lined with blunt needles that appear lacy and fine. And in a strong enough breeze, the knobby branches furl back, exposing pale undersides that look inviting and soft.

The trees have always been a part of this landscape, companions on shaded ridges and alongside cool rivers. Such fondness makes it hard to accept that they might one day be gone, and I brush one as I pass, for the comfort of its smell. I have no idea how old the tree is, as it's impossible to estimate hemlock age based on height. The species can tolerate shade, which means that for decades they might barely grow, until at last there is light—a neighboring tree dies or is taken down by a saw or storm—and the hemlock undergoes a growth spurt, pushing high into the upper story. Only a core sample can reveal the actual age, and on some of these hard-to-reach slopes, researchers are discovering trees more than four hundred years old.

Little else in these woods can compare with that life span; few other species contain so many tales. A tree of that age knew the native peoples who once traveled this land, along with the elk and wolves and mile-long flocks of passenger pigeons. A four-hundred-year-old hemlock witnessed the first carts and carriages, the earliest

tractors and trolleys and trains. It felt the vibrations of
rifles and church bells, chainsaws and waterwheels, and
jets traveling so fast they cracked sound waves above it.
It experienced years when snow fell every month, when
ash from distant volcanoes coated its limbs, and when
prolonged droughts made it retreat into stunned and
dormant states. It watched as the surrounding hills were
stripped of trees and then left to grow into forest again,
and it felt the pressure of acid rain, of a thinning ozone
layer, of the sheer weight of human life pressing down
on the planet.

Yet its rich trove of stories is about to cease gathering.
A new and tiny parasite has appeared on the scene, as
lethal as the other waves of disease to pass this way, HIV
and the various cancers that are felling friends like Karl.

The hemlock's bane—woolly adelgids—recently arrived from Japan, where two insect predators kept them
in check. But here, according to Karl, the hemlocks are
defenseless, and all of them may be gone within the next
ten or so years. We will know the adelgids have taken
hold when bits of white wool appear on the branches,
or when nymphs stream from the eggs in April or May,
sucking sap as they travel through tender new needles.
Once the tree has been infested, vital sap drawn from its
core, it dies a slow death, from its limbs to the crown.
Four years, Karl said, is the typical life span once adelgids have begun to suck. He had less than a year.

I don't know how we'll mourn the hemlocks' passing,
whether we will have organized laments on town com-
mons or retreat into private moments. It's not as though
we haven't had practice; we know what it's like to have a
landscape of skeletons, left after disease decimated both
the chestnuts and elms. But it takes time to get used to

an emptied space, a chair suddenly vacant at the table, a phone that will no longer be answered. Each loss seems to ratchet up the risk we take when falling in love with someone new.

In the remains of the fire, where all day we tossed branches left each time Jack felled and limbed a tree, the coals can still scorch flesh. I rake partially burned limbs into the orange bed of heat and have to step back to keep my face from blistering. A few feet away, the temperature is about ten degrees below zero, which feels warmer than during the day because the gusts have lessened at last. In their wake, the air is bitter and dry, the stars sharp overhead.

Trees snap in the distance and a dog barks down in the village, yet a deep quiet keeps the sounds from resonating. I can see a few house lights to the south, but otherwise I am alone, in a circle of fire-lit snow not far from the edge of the woods.

I remember Jack's earlier talk about fear, which surprised me coming from a man who handles six thousand pounds of oxen, though in this case it was a fear of heights. We had been watching as my nephew, an agile tree climber, strapped a harness around his waist, attached spikes to his boots, and hoisted himself into the trees, a chainsaw dangling from his belt. His pruning helped ensure that the trees fell where we wanted, instead of tangling in the branches of those growing too closely together.

"I can't look any longer," Jack had said, "or for sure I'll get sick." He turned his back and kept talking about other things that unsettled him, such as trees with vertical limbs that make it hard to tell where they will fall or big coyotes appearing in places where they had never lived before. "Damn but change just isn't easy," he said.

My bones ache from dragging and stacking pine branches all day, though since sunset I have simply tended the fire as it died down, taking increasingly long breaks inside our warm house. But on this last trip of the day, I lean on the rake and begin to feel that I am not alone after all. The heat and the glow are too strong, the skitter of sparks too curious to ignore. It's then that I imagine a line of animals on the ridge, hidden just behind the distant line of trees—the fisher, whose tracks I followed a few days ago; the foxes that raised kits in a nearby den last spring; the short-tailed weasel I watched as it bounded across the brook; the coyote who traipsed through last fall.

I imagine the careful distance they keep from each other, wary of me but unafraid of the pop of sparks. I think of their patience, and how long they can sit, and the fact that, though they feel some hunger, it is the heat they are after. Their newness in this place and to each other doesn't matter.

It's too frigid to imagine otherwise; it's increasingly hard to breathe. I sense that as soon as I scrape the last pine chunks into the hot center and begin the uphill walk to the house, they will inch their way down. They will come closer and closer, gaining access to the coals that will warm them all night, or at least slow the loss of their own store of warmth. In the process, they will also inspect the oxen's trail and sniff out what we have done and discover how exposed they are now that much of the cover is gone.

And though I can't see them, I have a vague sense of why it is I want them here—somehow fixing this moment of flux with other living things, while sharing this last gift of the pines on the coldest night of the year. And then it's too cold to imagine anything at all, and I slog for the last time up the hill to the house.

Rescue

A WHITE WEASEL SHIMMIES through brown woods, ladybugs stroll on the outside of the window, and winter keeps surprising us, this time for its odd warmth. We should have a cover of snow by now; ermine and insects should not be visible. But their very presence suggests that more curiosities await us, so when a friend comes to visit, a newcomer to this area, I'm quick to suggest a walk along the Deerfield River, on the same path once walked by the Mahican and the Mohawk.

A sudden flurry of snow spills over us as we cross rock-strewn slopes of hemlock and laurel, through open woods of oak and maple. Though it's Geoff's first time in New England, he knows the landscape by heart, having traveled it again and again through the work of Robert Frost. "Out through the fields and the woods / And over the walls I have wended . . ."

He finishes the stanza as we balance on log bridges and pick up stones to see what might have life underneath. We take turns reciting other Frost favorites and then begin "Birches" together, as though we had planned it, as though we're both there with the boy who became expert at choosing and climbing a tree, learning to swing out at just the right moment, the birch strong enough to hold him and limber enough to arc over with his weight, before lowering him to earth again.

I tell Geoff that I had done the same as a kid and convinced my youngest sister to try it, too, the rushing down far too fast after the buildup of the climb, but not so fast that it deterred me from doing it again and again, and Geoff declares he wants to do it, he always has. He's lean and quite tall, and it'll be a challenge to find a tree that can both hold this grown man and give way. It's a curious tension that he himself couldn't manage—to be firm as well as yield—when a literary award freed him to explore new options, and he left his wife and job and home and took to the road and the poets' retreats. The boy in him still believes all is possible, however, and that same boy emerges now, boisterous and joyful, knocking on hollow logs and flipping over more stones, eager to discover what else might live in these woods.

And then we're stopped by a beaver lodge tucked into the river's bank.

Such a foolish place to build! Beaver can't affect this setting, the way they can with a slower stream. This will never be that marshy place made for ducks and frogs and great blue herons, for dragonflies and sleepy turtles. The valley is too steep and rugged, the river too violent in two of its four seasons. These may be teenaged beaver, kits kicked out by the new brood's arrival, too naïve to know they can't slow a river. Or they wandered these parts too late in the season to find a waterway better suited to their needs. Or perhaps all the good brooks were already taken and this was where winter, not desire, made them stop.

The choicest sites are at a premium—if the number counters are right. According to one report, about seventy thousand beaver now live in Massachusetts, four times what there were just ten years ago, a boom due to the state's new ban on leghold traps. The audible awe heard in the voices of those who watch them shove mud and topple trees, teeth and a tail all the tools that they need, make clear that few humans want to interfere with this feat.

For my part, I would like to think aesthetics detoured them here, where the river stretches broad and wide after the upstream tumble of falls and dams. A powerful quiet surrounds us in this 20 degree air, and I feel muffled and held by the swirl of soft snow, though if Geoff weren't here, on this very gray day, I would probably feel very alone.

That sense of aloneness may be the best reason for this beaver's choice of home. The sulfuric acid spill that happened late last summer took place just six miles north on the North River. The heaver-than-water toxin surged along the river's bottom, dissolving every fish in its way, until a beaver dam stopped it. That gave the Department of Environmental Protection team time to rush in and neutralize the spill with great quantities of baking soda. In the accident's aftermath, however, no one knew the health or whereabouts of the beavers, though we all wanted to assume they had lit out for safer territory.

This may be the home of the very same animals, the ones that inadvertently saved a whole raft of lives.

Geoff calls at the lodge, though they won't show while we're here, and I tell him about another river rescue, one that happened when I was seven or eight years old. My mother had driven us to a local swimming hole, and, too hot and impatient to wait while she unpacked smaller kids from the car, I raced ahead and leapt into the river, expecting to hit bottom and spring back up again. But the water was deeper than I expected, my feet never touched, and I flailed for the surface and began swallowing river instead of air. I thrashed and couldn't stop myself and went down again and then somehow I was on the shore next to a soaking-wet stranger, my mother was rushing toward us as the woman backed away, and in the confusion no one had time to ask her for her name.

Sometimes, when I'm in a roomful of people, I look around and wonder if she's among them, the person who jumped in to save a drowning child and then had to rush away, embarrassed by her sopping dress and flattened hair. For his part, Geoff grins at all we can't know about strangers and beavers and then he's off, leaping from rock to rock, and I amble slowly after, still watching for a birch tree large enough for him to climb and thin enough to sweep him back to earth.

Salamander Crossing

I ONCE PICKED UP a child from the roadside, a boy I
had never seen before in a town I rarely passed through.
A friend and I were driving toward Camel's Hump in
northern Vermont for a day of hiking while the leaves
were just ideas and the views big and unimpeded. But
first there was the crying child on the grass, his bike on its
side, pieces of metal strewn around him. He let us check
the knee he held, a nasty scrape already bubbling blood.

We packed him into the car and drove him up a hill
far too steep for rickety wheels and a scared seven-year-
old in a snowsuit, a bulky knapsack on his back. Once at
his house, we knocked until his mother appeared, disheveled and in a bathrobe, holding the screen door closed
between us. She looked beaten and suspicious, her hair
awry, dark circles under her eyes. I imagine she would
have hit him if we hadn't stayed there, waiting. "He's a
brave kid," I said. "He almost made it." I looked back at
the yard and didn't see any vehicles. "Do you want us to
drop him off at school?"

She didn't. "We'll manage," she said.

I took my time retrieving bike parts from the car, arranging them on the lawn, piecing together the story

out of the snuffling he had done earlier. He had waited and waited until he was sure he had missed his bus and, knowing better than to wake her, he took off the fastest way possible. It takes a moment to realize that his bus hadn't come when he expected it because the clocks had been switched to daylight savings overnight, and, since no one in the house had remembered, the kid was left to do his best on the bike.

We left; we climbed the mountain, and all day I felt oddly off, as though I could float over long stretches of rock, miscalculate distances, or become distracted and forget to get off the summit before dark. As though being an hour out of time meant we could be knocked off the path, if we didn't pay close attention to our feet and our speed.

It happens every spring. We jerk ourselves out of the rhythms that surround us, just when the hours of sunlight seem long enough to approximate our days, just when it's easy to sense the exact moment of sunrise, the exact place on the horizon where it sets. Then daylight savings comes around and we have to learn the patterns all over again.

For the first week or two afterward, I feel tugged two ways at once, though it's most noticeable at night. During the day, there's school and appointments and work around the house, and no choice but to pay attention to clock ticks and digital flashings. But after dark, through windows opened at last, spring comes at us like a train, and it's lusty and oblivious to whether or not we're groggy or wholly in our bodies. Its throbbing goes on until dawn, chaotic and barely contained—the spiraling woodcock, the quacking wood frog, the ruffed grouse on his log, slamming wings against air, like a line of cancan dancers, exacting and violent.

Much of the new life is easy to see—fists of skunk cabbage, swollen streams, green spikes shooting up from underground bulbs. It takes a different kind of attention to know that other groundswell, the bodies that slip and blat their way through the woods, across roads, past new construction sites, old stone walls, the driven and unstoppable frogs and toads and salamanders, heading for a vernal pool and a night of urgent coupling.

It's a journey I first saw when driving home one foggy night in March—a large salamander stumping across the road, its shape distorted by the glint of headlights off its damp body. Just beyond it was another and then another and another, all of them so big and sudden they looked prehistoric. I had to stop the car. I had to wonder how much I'd had to drink. Then I had to get a closer look— spotted salamanders, four and five inches long, with yellow dots all along their black bodies, and too focused on their goal to be deterred by the car's lights or my height. They may have moved faster but they didn't change course. The rain fell harder; it was cold; I wanted to get home, but there were all these salamanders in the road.

And countless others in the woods all around us— marbled and Jefferson's and blue-spotted salamanders; spring peepers and gray tree frogs; green and pickerel frogs; American and Fowler's toads. Several thousand wood frogs in one pool alone. Maybe even a spadefoot toad, though it's the rarest, its reproductive cycle so fast it can complete the whole affair in one night—emerging from its underground chamber and heading for a pool, crying out and finding a ready mate, and then releasing the eggs if female or fertilizing them if male. Within hours, the eggs morph into embryos; within days they hatch; within two to three weeks, small toadlets stretch their legs and hop through the woods, equipped with all they need to dig their own burrows.

One month, total, from conception to first apartment. Others take longer, traveling single file or in processions, as predictable as the shift of constellations across the sky. A warm, wet night at the end of March or early April and they're off, pulled through the night to the pool they first knew, that large puddle in the woods that teems with life for a month or two—tadpoles, fingernail clams, fairy shrimp, and the turtles and raccoons and wading birds that arrive to eat them—and then all is gone, dried up, leaf-littered.

Where the paths of these migrants cross busy roads, there's carnage, thousands of flattened skins left behind by morning. Some towns have responded by closing those roads for the few late-night hours when amphibians are on the move. Others have constructed tunnels to funnel salamanders safely under, while in a few nearby areas, volunteers provide the escort service, citizens in boots and raincoats, schlepping small creatures across busy byways.

A breeze blows out of the south in a night still chilly with the melting of ice and the telephones start ringing, the network of calls like the croaking of frogs, connecting strangers with flashlights in this urgent, wet ritual. We're sleepy; we're slickered; we're in a moment out of time as we abet hastening salamanders to that place, so easy to imagine, where desire and relief meet at last.

Disquiet

1.

Strands of barbed wire loop from tree to tree or dangle in short pieces from scarred bark. Remnants of stone-walls outline the sites of former farms and suggest that rocks were the early settlers' biggest crop. Rising to either side of the dirt path are ridges littered with caves, where mountain lions—known here as catamounts—once wandered. So did the Scots-Irish Methodists who tilled these lands years ago and held services in one of the bigger caves until their own church was built.

I continue past the cellar holes, my goal the body of water at the top of this climb, fifty acres of lake in the middle of Catamount State Forest. I hadn't expected, however, to be quite so alone. I'm less than a mile from the nearest home, barely two from the state highway, and there's no one around and no sounds of any kind— no cars or trucks, no trains or planes, no dogs or crows or chainsaws. Such absence feels palpable, as though I've stumbled into an oddly stalled moment in time.

Then the ease of walking takes over, the rhythm frees me into other places, and I find myself thinking about my great-great-grandfather Judson Ford, whose journal

I've been reading, after a cousin found and gave it to my father this past year. Ford was keeping the journal, he notes on the book's first page, as a way to help improve his lot in life, which, in the 1850s, seemed otherwise fairly limited. ("There are three great events in one's history," he writes, without irony, "to become a Christian, to become a married man, and to die.") When he can get away from his job at the print shop, he goes to concerts, museums, and lectures, including one, "Popery Unmasked," which he describes at some length.

I pause on the trail to listen, sure I heard the voice of another person, but the only sound is the dribble of brook over stones. Discomfort with Judson Ford must have stopped me, though this relative's distaste for "popery" should come as no surprise. Anti-Catholic fervor was rampant in the mid-nineteenth century, and he was riding its wave. The "unmasking" lecturer, whom he doesn't name, had managed to gain access to "convents, nunneries and abominable Inquisition Rooms and . . . witnessed there scenes too cruel and barbarous to be credited." Catholics, the lecturer had impressed on his audience, were diabolical, primitive people.

For a while this father of my father's grandmother, who died just after she was born, was so swept up in local protests that he joined the Native American Party, a group angered by the growing numbers of Irish immigrants. He voted the entire nativist slate in a subsequent election and made careful note in his diary of his candidates' advances, along with the disappointing news that none of them had won. The same bias persists, though softened by the press of comradeship, in an entry made on his first night as a new soldier for the Union Army. He and a few other men had organized an evening prayer

and Bible reading, which went off quite well, "considering that there were only half a dozen Christians present
and many of the balance were swearing Irish."

It's a curious reminder that, had Holly and I been
alive then, our religions rather than our lesbian iden-
tities might have been the biggest obstacle to our relationship. As an Irish Catholic child attending parochial
school, she was warned against people like me—Protes-
tants doomed to hell, according to her teachers, and so
confused about God that they kept splintering into ever-
odder denominations. That she has joined her life to a
member of the forbidden class—and a public school girl,
at that—sometimes shocks her sensibilities as much as
I did that Ash Wednesday when I stuck my thumb into
an ashtray and glibly marked both our foreheads. *Blas-
phemer!* she howled, her strained laughter giving away
just how much she would suffer for it.

The trail levels off amid a thick stand of white pine and
soon ends in a great stretch of dark water. Around the
lake, between large granite outcrops, swamp maples
flare crimson while sugar maples have begun their turn
to yellow and orange. From what I've learned of Judson
Ford, scenes like these gave him great pleasure, his entries splendid in their details after an afternoon spent
skating on the Charles River, or fishing in Boston Har-
bor, or traipsing from dawn to dusk along trails in the
White Mountains. And while passion appears in other
entries as well, as in the scheme he and his brother con-
coct for locating potential wives ("we have determined
to do our 'courting' without the knowledge of the other
party") or in his accounts of the "terrible excitement"

building among Yankees against the Southern "traitors," they can't compare with those that embody his love of the outdoors.

His desires, in fact, seem very much like my own, particularly in the last letter he wrote to his brother, six months after enlisting with the Cambridge Volunteers. His regiment had been sent to North Carolina, where they had yet to see action, and he spent time identifying some of the blossoming flowers and trees around him. The wait for war and lushness of spring feed a dream he's long held, and he writes wistfully of finding a place where he can raise a family, far from the city and the dark printing office. "O how many times I have longed, since I have got used to outdoor life and hard knocks, to have the chance open up before me, when I return, to go upon a farm and stay there the rest of my days . . . Do you think there is any hope for me in respect to my becoming a farmer?"

He didn't live long enough to receive his brother's reply. The next scrap of paper tucked inside the book is the notice of his death two months later from typhoid fever.

I sit on a long slope of rock, glad for the moments of bright sun between gusts of cold wind. Each blast is brief, a fast shirring of water and then it's over and I can again see a newt shimmy through weeds.

And yet the stillness crowds closer, so that it's not a breeze on my neck but an eerie lifting of hairs. Other than the chucking of a distant chipmunk, I hear no other animals, nor can I see the movement of any insects or birds, and I don't know why. Usually I welcome silence, but this quiet is uncanny, like the stillness right after a winter storm, when the wind has stopped at last, a blanket of snow covers everything, and no birds or animals have yet ventured forth.

I cast about for explanations. We're only two days past the equinox and still six weeks from first snow; we haven't yet had a killing frost. Perhaps hilltops in autumn are simply less attractive than valleys, which are rife now with berries and insects and seeds. Or perhaps the lake's pH is changing, making it less hospitable to living things, downwind as it is from coal-fired plants in the Midwest. Or perhaps this is an inkling of what climate change will look like, with altered habitats and weather patterns affecting animal species everywhere.

In the stillness, I feel dislocated, unsure of my footing. I can't help but think of things insidious and invisible, like radioactive emissions from the nearby nuclear power plant. Though it's in the process of being decommissioned, its guts shipped elsewhere, more than five hundred spent fuel rods still sit in pools of water, awaiting the building of the federal government's promised storage facility. I can't help but wonder what half-lives tick down here, what sorts of atoms might have drifted over in the winds or ground waters.

And then I have to head home, unsure how to assess what seems unnatural about the place or why silence can be so disquieting.

2.

The Mohawk Trail—State Route 2—twists and climbs up into the Berkshire Mountains, makes a sharp hairpin turn that drivers regularly miss, hitting the restaurant at the curve so often that the owners finally moved it, then drops into the town of North Adams. A series of mills once flourished here, but all of the industry either fled or folded, leaving behind an impoverished landscape. The decay stands in stark contrast to affluent Williamstown, the next town to the west and home to Williams College and the Clark Art Institute. But it's in North Adams' abandoned brick mill buildings that the state's Museum of Contemporary Art has made a home, as much an aberration as is its current theme, "Unnatural Science." The large installation Holly and I have come to see seems more appropriate to the nearby college than to the life of the factories—Michael Oatman's re-creation of the workplace of Henry Perkins, a University of Vermont zoologist from 1902 to 1945 and onetime director of its natural history museum—until one gets close enough to read the writing.

The space, which smells of leather and old documents, features charts on the walls, stacks of slides on the desk, and books and boxes of artifacts arrayed around the room. In addition to depicting Perkins's studies and habits, Oatman has made a visual history of an idea that went badly awry. Under the silhouettes of misshapen people are the terms Perkins used to identify *morons* and *misfits* and *cripples*. Family trees, mapped out on the walls, include the *feebleminded* and *criminal*, the *wanton* and *immoral*.

Fifty years earlier, Irish Catholics might have topped the order, but here it's the *non-pure* Vermonters that are the more numerous, including French Canadians, Abenaki Indians, and houseboat dwellers on Lake Champlain, along with alcoholics, battered women, and the poor. Defect fascinated him, as did the way it was inherited, and Perkins soon founded the Eugenics Survey of Vermont, determined to eliminate such problems at their source.

According to many of these early eugenicists, the principles of animal husbandry were easily applied to people. Every farmer knows the importance of selecting healthy stock to mate; it's the only sure way to achieve sturdy, viable offspring. The practice when applied to humans is just as simple, the world is better for it, and children, in particular, stand a greater chance of success in the otherwise grim life that awaits them.

Having determined the rates at which degenerate families were multiplying (numbers later proven to be wildly inaccurate), Perkins calculated the high costs incurred in caring for their offspring, data he and his team of social workers used to appeal to a lot of thoughtful Vermonters. It was the moral imperative of decent citizens, Perkins claimed, to defend themselves and their children against the spread of faulty *geneplasm,* which, left unchecked, would continue to produce the lawless and mentally defective. The most straightforward way to do this—to protect the security and pursuit of happiness of the moral and law-abiding—was to sterilize unfit breeders.

By the mid-1930s, Vermont, along with thirty-two other states, had enacted sterilization legislation, due in part to Perkins's findings. Nationwide, some sixty thousand people were sterilized as a result of eugenics laws, though the actual numbers may have been far higher. Then Hitler took race cleansing to a horrifying extreme, and most U.S. citizens couldn't distance themselves fast enough from eugenics societies.

We leave Oatman's installation and continue past other exhibits, all focused in some way on the unnatural in nature. But a new story has arisen between me and them, one my grandmother recently told and that I'm now hearing in a different way, about the time her father, as one of the selectmen of a small town in Maine, had to deliver a local boy to the state hospital for a vasectomy. According to my grandmother, who sensed that she was the only family member who ever knew the whole story, her father had no choice. The boy was strong, he had begun assaulting girls, and his IQ was too low for him to understand what he was doing. And yet the mix of pain and obligation her father must have felt still showed on her face, eighty years later, along with the burden of silence the two of them carried.

What her face didn't register was a sense of why I might care about this, too. She was back in other memories of precious times with her dad, and I was left to remember how often people like Perkins attached *defective* and *immoral* to *homosexual*.

3.

On a gray winter day, I strap on snowshoes to walk again into the Catamount Hills. About a quarter mile up, in the middle of the trail, a half-eaten gray squirrel looks frozen mid-scold. It's covered with just enough of last night's snow that I can't tell what killed or carried it. Farther on, an animal has walked along fallen logs before struggling with something, a circle of old blood in the snow; in its midst I find a bobcat print, so well defined it must have been made within the last few hours.

It's probably the cat's mark that makes me feel watched, the drag of my snowshoes loud to any quiet thing on the ridge, so many cracks and hollows from which to peer, and nothing for me to see but shadow. The bobcat's presence might also account for the increasing quiet around me, though with unnatural science on my

mind and insidious influences all around, I can easily
conjure other reasons.

Before I can develop them, however, the saucer-sized
prints of a bear cross my path and I immediately start
after them, up the hill to my right. I can't keep from slipping at the steep angle, so I strip off what I don't need—
water bottle, scarf, snowshoes—and then I'm climbing,
grabbing roots and rocks to keep from tumbling downhill, amazed at the bear's speed, its vertical ascent.

I can't see beyond the rocks in front of me and have
no idea what might lie beyond. But when I reach a narrow plateau, I see no scurrying, hulking bear. It's simply
a place to pause and breathe before the next steep climb,
an area laced with deer tracks and those of one bounding
bear. I keep on, careful to step where it did, where I'm
more likely to get good purchase on loose rocks under
the snow. But I am far clumsier than it and leave more
skid marks on the downhill slope.

Then both feet slide out from under me, and I catch
a branch before falling and dangle above a long drop. I
aim my feet toward what looks like deep snow and let go.
The impact isn't bad, and as I brush myself off, I notice
cave openings all around, the entrances of some barred
with thick icicles, the low hang of others suggesting rank
and tight chambers, and I wish I understood how a bear
thinks. I don't know why a bear is out and about in January, and not bundled into sleep, which is what bears do in
the winter, particularly colder-than-normal winters like
the one we're having now. It's how bears are designed,
with their thick fur and stored fat and ability to slow
their heart and lungs to half their summertime speeds.
Unless they're suffering duress, as was the one Edward
Hoagland once described, a bear that had been shot with

a .22, leaving the animal alive but in such pain that it couldn't settle anywhere. It moved repeatedly through the winter, den to den, until it finally died. The person who found it cut it open and discovered the bear's swollen belly full of undigested blood.

I want the bear I'm following to be sturdy and strong and only out of its den because something startled it, though a bobcat is too small, and coyotes too smart. A wolf might dislodge it, but there hasn't been a wild one here since the mid-1800s. A catamount might bedevil it, though they too have long been gone, unless the rumored sightings are true, and it's here that they're staging a comeback.

Along the ridge, deer have ambled casually, their zigzagging paths showing no evidence of worry, and the bear has looped around here, too, its trail a wide circle along the knoll before abruptly dropping downhill. I opt to follow. The bear slides; I slide. The bear vaults an ice-locked stream; I leap and land in its tracks. It scurries under wiry laurel branches; I bend and do the same. On we go, a dislodged bear and me, the pieces behind revealing our differences—the branches I break, the dark hairs it left, our strides alternately short and long.

And then we're again to the old town road, not far from where I first left the trail. The bear has wandered back the way it came, over a frozen swamp and into a dense growth of spruce that I could only fit through on my hands and knees. That's when I quit, though I reassure myself that I'll return soon, with time enough to walk until the trail ends and ideas enough to figure out why it's roaming about this cold time of year.

In the time I do have, I retrieve my snowshoes and continue on to the lake. It's another twenty minutes of fast walking before I realize that again I'm surrounded by deep quiet and that even the number of deer tracks has been reduced to a single animal's. I step onto the granite ledge overlooking the snow-covered lake and hear nothing but the shiver of dry beech leaves. Nothing else moves. Nothing sighs. Nothing calls out. Once again I have the feeling that something here isn't quite natural. I want to see a red squirrel flinging cone parts or a flock of pine grosbeaks feeding under low branches. I want to hear a raven, a woodpecker, an animal moving along the higher ridge. But when nothing appears and my sweat starts to feel cold, I realize I'm having to rethink what "natural" means. I haven't quite got the pulse of this piece of land. I only know small pieces—a bear up and about in January, a nearby facility that generated nuclear power, a decline in bird numbers everywhere, and a growing sense that this is part of a far larger puzzle. With the dark coming early, I turn around and head home.

I arrive just as Holly returns from work and begin telling her where I've been and all I've seen. Her face freezes as I start listing details. "Following a bear?" she says. "My God, what's *wrong* with you? What if something happened? How would I have found you?"

She has a point, of course. I left no note and no one knew my plans. Though what I really want to tell her, and fortunately have all night to do so, is that it's actually quite natural to track an errant bear and its story. I don't know how else to make sense of all these changes we're living through or how best to prepare ourselves for what's still to come.

Hitched, Massachusetts, 2004

WE WAIT IN THE OFFICE, the two of us, on narrow metal chairs, the first time I have shared a doctor's appointment with another adult. In the silence after the nurse leaves, the idea of us, in this small room, in this rural corner of the state, is almost enough to make me bolt. Old butch-femme roles loom over us, like some caricature of the husband-wife model that has shaped every legal wedding ever to take place in this country, and all because Holly is in a linen blouse and nice pants, dressed for this afternoon's end-of-the-semester party at Smith College, where she now works, while I'm in worn jeans and ratty sneakers, ready to return to the garden on this lovely day off. Yet our dress, these chairs, this curious waiting—they also conjure a discomfiting scene from years ago, when I was painting boats in a shipyard and my partner was a well-paid therapist making ten times my hourly rate, and she sauntered into the house one day, outfitted in conference elegance, and announced that the groceries were in the trunk, expecting—and knowing—that I would bring them in. Our relationship probably began unraveling at that moment.

Today's situation is not the same at all—we're old
enough (and healed enough) to do things because we
want to, not because our significant others expect it—
but then another scene appears while we wait for this
premarital exam to take place, of a wedding I once happened upon at a gay bar, somewhere in New Jersey, with
tuxes and slicked-back coifs on the groom and her en-
tourage, and plenty of makeup and big hair on the bride
and her attendants. They looked so convincing I thought
I had the wrong place, until I began to see other people
in the room who looked like me.

Now, however, mostly free of the cultural ideals about
how women should look and act and attend to their bodies, we're faced with a new challenge: liberating ourselves
from notions of "wife" and "wife" and/or "husband." It's
as though the very act of sitting together in this room,
ready to answer a series of questions before our blood is
drawn, links us with every heterosexual union that ever
preceded us. There is no model for how two women go
through this process; there are simply the steps necessary for intended couples in the Commonwealth of Massachusetts, the first of which is proof that neither of us
has syphilis.

The nurse-practitioner asks about our general health
and listens to our hearts. My body tells it all: Despite my
jeans and muscles, my would-be tough stance, my pulse
is hammering away about 20 percent faster than usual.

I'm getting married and I'm not sure what to make
of it.

She sticks my arm, and I look away, and when she
does the same to Holly, I pace the hallway, looking everywhere but there. "It's so exciting," she says then, and
clearly she means it (though she claims the sudden color

in her face is from a weekend sunburn). "Suddenly everyone in town has a fiancée."

On the way home, we stop in the village and saunter down the sidewalk, wanting someone to see our matching Band-Aids, wanting someone to ask how we are. When Christin pulls up on her three-speed bike, her long red hair taking longer to come to a stop, we tell her the news and confess to mixed feelings. "It's not surprising," she says in an effort to be reassuring. "Normal people have them, too."

By Christin's definition, "not-normal" is where I've long been, an outlaw because of who I love, not because I sought out the identity. And then, of course, I liked the role. There's a certain freedom to being put outside the law, in a region without rules. There's an adrenaline rush that comes with flagrance, a giddiness with being reckless. *We* get to decide how we love and how we show it. *We* get to make up the rules and know they might change tomorrow.

At the same time, we're never quite free of reminders of all we can't choose, which, in the world of marriage, number about one thousand from which gays and lesbians are excluded. Health insurance, pension plans, tax deductions, Medicaid, survivorship and social security benefits—those have become rewards granted to straight wedded couples. Yet, despite the fact that we too create warm homes, and tend each other through fevers and surgeries, and take turns staying strong when people we love die or when children are threatened or when nightmares cut through our sleep, our union isn't recognized by state or federal governments. We are ineligible for family leave, for guaranteed hospital visitation or access to intensive care units, for spousal (lower) rates on car insurance, travel fares, or packaged vacation plans. We aren't included in "a family's right to know" in legal or health matters, nor are we protected from having to testify against each other in court. We aren't even permitted to eat the lobsters the other might catch, unless both of us have purchased similar fishing licenses. (A straight person with the proper license can share the haul with anyone in his or her family.)

That leaves us denied, shut out, occasionally belligerent, or working extra hard to prove our lives are truly no different from anyone else's. We dance between the twin impulses, as the feminist scholar Catharine Stimpson once put it, of transgression and domesticity. We want to be bad, and we want to shack up. We like our exemption from stifling codes of conformity, and we want to cuddle and make nests, like the billions of lovers before us. The "urge to merge" that runs rampant among lesbians—captured in the old joke about the U-Haul that a lesbian brings on the second date—means we dive into the sharing of lives and clothes, beds and dreams. We even mutter "Marry me" in intimate moments, as though the verb were the only word powerful enough to convey the urgency of our love.

But then, like a good outlaw—and here I have to differentiate from Holly, who lived a married life for two decades with a Cuban husband—I often mocked the idea of marriage. It's a deed, not a license, I would say; it subsumes a woman into a man's name and property, which makes it tough to find female friends after they surrender their identity. It's a capitalist extravaganza, a huge expense for a few hours of showtime, a setup for years of imbalance. Marriage, I would point out, ups the degree of difficulty for any woman who wants to find her own way in a world that gives men first dibs on almost everything.

Of course, not all lesbians I know heaped such scorn on the practice; some romanced their way right into the ritual—gay weddings that looked like straight weddings, with the same music and outfits and cake designs, and dinner and dancing and a honeymoon afterward. Others opted for a civil union or commitment ceremony, a way to make their love public and widen the circle of support in a world rarely kind to nonconformists, especially to those who express their difference sexually.

Others adopted a more blasé response and decided they didn't care. So what if straight women can marry in front of hundreds of people and receive tons of gifts and have doors and career paths opened as a consequence? So what if saying someone is married is the fastest short-hand in most social situations? So what if such women never have to pause on the form that instructs us to "check one—single, married, divorced, widowed"?

Who really cares? At least, who spent much time caring about it until Massachusetts' highest court ruled in November 2003 that the state's constitution guaranteed equality for all its citizens, and that gay couples could no longer be excluded from the institution of marriage? I sure didn't. Yet the subsequent turn of events has made it seem unavoidable.

According to the justices, anything short of marriage would "confer an official stamp of approval on the destructive stereotype that same-sex relationships are inherently unstable and inferior to opposite-sex relationships and are not worthy of respect." The court gave the legislature 180 days to remedy the injustice, reminding lawmakers that "the benefits accessible by way of marriage license are enormous, touching nearly every aspect of life and death." May 17, 2004, they said, is when gay marriages can begin taking place.

Which left us in a quandary. If the legislature didn't derail the court's ruling, would we take advantage of the option and marry?

For months we avoided answering the question.

The forms are so new, the town clerk can't find them in the five minutes she spends looking. She knows the envelope is somewhere in the room, but what with the town celebrating its 225th birthday, and organizing for the festivities taking so much of her time, she hasn't been able to keep up with all the paperwork. Fortunately, the clerk in the next town finds hers and she faxes Janice a copy.

We sit across from her at a table near where the Select Board meets, its weekly sessions standard fare on the local cable-access network. She hands us pens and cheerily asks when the wedding will be. We hesitate before answering; we have so little practice in using the words. "We don't think of it as a wedding," I say. "It's simply a civil marriage, a legal deal." The gladness fades from her face, and we bend our heads to look over the new form. I become Party A, Holly becomes Party B, terms that replace *bride* and *groom*, and we fill in every line, while Janice describes the safer subject—a recent town parade and fireworks, and how great the weather was.

We tell her we're sorry we missed it, but we were attending a wedding in Miami. We don't tell her the specifics—that it was a traditional, Catholic wedding. That we sat between our son, Rudy (Holly's by her first marriage), and his wife, Yuri, who got married during their lunch hour, and in the row in front of our daughter, Chandra (Holly's by her first marriage), and her husband, Freddy, who got married in the grand style, six months of preparation before the actual event, and then the two of them like movie stars in an almost perfectly scripted event—except that Chandra's father and his wife refused to come, which meant her brother gave her away, and then there we were, her mom and me, walking down the aisle behind her after the ceremony was done.

Nor do we tell the town clerk about what happened before we left Miami on this more recent trip, when the six of us sat together in the living room, the ball game finally ended, and I muted the television, signaling huge news in the offing. Holly cleared her throat, I cleared mine, the four of them watching our every facial shift.

"We're planning to get married," we said, "in a legal ceremony, just the two of us and a JP, so don't worry, you don't have to make plans to be there. It's going to be simple and brief, a civil marriage because we think it's the right thing to do and because of the legal protections and because in the long run we think it's good for all of us."

At first I couldn't read the expressions on their faces, and then Chandra clapped! Freddy hurried to get a bottle of champagne, and Rudy offered a toast but almost couldn't say the words because of how choked up he was, while next to him, Yuri nodded and smiled.

We flew home two days later, May 17, the fiftieth anniversary of *Brown v. Board of Education*, the landmark ruling that made clear that separate was not equal when it came to public education and that schools had to be integrated forthwith. We crossed the state line close to midnight, entering our small and radical commonwealth in the last minutes of its big day. Ten hours later, we were at the town clerk's office just as she arrived to conduct the morning's business.

Holly says the new marriage law is like a fire sale on rights. *New York Times* columnist David Brooks uses similar language, though mockingly at first. Liberals, he writes, make gay marriage sound "like a really good employee benefits plan. Or they frame it as a civil rights issue, like extending the right to vote."

To Brooks, marriage is no routine or laughing matter; it's a serious and threatened institution, and it's fast becoming a contract of *contingency*, with little remaining emphasis on the original agreement of *fidelity*. In a position that seems surprising, given his regular defense of Republican values, he writes that it's going to fall to conservatives "to make the important, moral case for marriage." And that, he insists, means including gay marriage. Allowing gays to marry, he implies, will help restore a critical emphasis on faithfulness.

Another columnist, Ellen Goodman, spent much of May 17 interviewing some of the couples waiting in line at town offices. "There are few cynics applying for licenses in this wedding week," she wrote afterward in the *Boston Globe*. The palpable part for her—in addition to sensing all the jitters—was the similarity between gay and straight couples when it came to creating caring units that looked a whole lot like every other family she knew. "In Massachusetts, same sex couples are now

choosing and celebrating the freedom," she wrote, paus-
ing with a long dash, "of commitment."

Like Brooks, she got it right, but only partly so, because there are lots of reasons besides fidelity and commitment that explain why queers might want to marry
and why doing so might cause palms to sweat. There's
no denying that when you pen your name to the marriage license or proclaim your love for another, you put
your integrity on the line, and we as a class of people are
not used to such public displays of intention. The whole
marriage license and subsequent ritual—or some queer-
equivalent of banns—says, to anyone within range, that I
will love, cherish, and do right by this particular person
for as long as I am alive and able.

That's a big package, but there is much more. As
women who love women, men who love men, we put our
very lives on the line as well: we risk being physically
targeted and emotionally abused, with nastiness ratch-
eted up to tense new levels, signs placed ever closer to
our homes—"God Abhors Fags." "Adam and Eve not
Adam and Steve." "There's a Reason God Gave Them
AIDS." Fortunately, most of us have had practice deal-
ing with homophobes.

Another, more dangerous, threat is one we inflict on
ourselves, the risk in believing we can *settle*, that this
new state of "normalcy" means we don't have to live outside the law any longer. And that, of course, means risk-
ing the dreaded state of complacency, a trait that plagues
every community that occupies a majority position in our
society. In the comfort of knowing we *belong*, we risk
forgetting what happens on the margins and in the dramas that helped shape and define us, and which continue
to be the narratives for other minority groups.

We also risk having this new contract stripped from us, as challenge after challenge enters the court system. With each legal battle, our lives are publicly examined all over again, which means neighbor facing neighbor, considering the odds.

But the biggest risk missed by both Brooks and Goodman—and one we skirt around, too—is the potential for serious injury to our hearts. Despite the best intentions of a small number of people in Massachusetts, the federal government refuses to recognize us, a result of the Defense of Marriage Act signed into law by President Clinton in 1996. If we let ourselves care too much about our new marriage status, we'll be bruised each time we run into the law of the land, which is written in a way that deliberately excludes us.

The three-day waiting period is up, and I breeze into the town hall to collect the license, glad for the banter with those who work in the building, people I worked alongside during my Planning Board tenure. In her small office, Janice shuffles papers and finds the certificate at last. She signs off, puts it into a preaddressed envelope, and hands it over. "A beautiful day we're having," she says.

I agree and then feel an odd silence as I leave. The town officials are suddenly busy with deskwork. No one looks up. No one says, "Congratulations." They opt instead for the old Yankee standby for behavior in awkward situations: Respect your neighbor's privacy and make no eye contact.

I don't open the envelope until I reach the car, and then there we are, our names inscribed on the form along

with those of our parents, and suddenly this feels far
more official than having a shared checking account or
owning a house together. This implicates the previous
generation. This says that we're about to be the queer
limb on the family tree and anyone doing a genealogi-
cal search will be able to see the way we have chosen to
declare what matters.

Which means soon we'll be the unit that "no man
can tear asunder," as was said at last Saturday's straight
wedding in Miami. We'll get deferential treatment—in
a few very small circles. We'll be guaranteed the right
to make medical decisions for each other, we'll be able
to check "married" on the next national census, and everything we own will go to the other when we die, unless
we specify otherwise in wills that we need to write soon.

We begin telling our straight friends, who can't make
sense of our reluctance to have a big party. They want
to put on nice clothes and eat good food and dance to a
klezmer band. They want to dip strawberries in chocolate and arrange flowers in fabulous bouquets and supply
a blessing, a ring bearer, a getaway vehicle.

They want us to know that they have accepted our
coupleness all along, that this really doesn't change anything, because really, they say, the two of you are already
as good as married. Yet still, they intimate, this changes
everything. This is what you have been denied for hundreds of years and now you can have it and we want to
stand up with you and why aren't you letting us?

We keep them at arm's length. It's not like that, we
tell them. It's about our hearts and the danger in letting this matter too much. To those who want to do

something we say, "No toasters, just toasts." After all, we explain, after the wedding takes place—if it does—we'll only be 1/50th citizens. Forty-nine states don't recognize our legal status, which means each time we leave Massachusetts, we'll be outlaws once again.

We have sixty days to take action before the marriage certificate expires, less than thirty before our blood tests will no longer be valid. We still have time to change our minds, and we consider backing out often, though now that we've agreed to do this with two other couples, we'll be considered traitors if we develop a case of cold feet. Besides, my short list of excuses—how to deal with the bizarre notion of "wife," or the difficulty in telling my ninety-nine-year-old grandmother, or the support this lends to the institution of the privileged—can't compare with the number of reasons to go through with this, which became longer with an unexpected Sunday-night phone call.

"As a father of two children," the automated voice begins, "I am horrified at the changes about to take place in our country." Despite my own horror, I don't hang up; I want a phone number, I want to register protest. "We urge you to support Article 8," the voice insists, describing a bill that will empower the legislature to repeal "activist judges" and prevent married homosexuals from tainting our nation's moral character.

Yet the specific judge that his group and others like it are targeting—Chief Justice Margaret Marshall—is my new hero, her moral fiber shaped by years in South Africa, where she actively fought her country's laws of apartheid and then had to emigrate to the States when it became too dangerous to stay in her homeland. One of the cases our chief justice likes to mention, when someone brings up the history of Massachusetts' Supreme Judicial Court (the oldest continuously running court in the western hemisphere) is that of Quock Walker, a slave who in 1781 ran away to work for a neighbor and was subsequently beaten when he was recaptured. He sued for assault, basing his case on the constitutional provision that "all men are created equal," and the SJC ruled in his favor, arguing that he was, in fact, a man, and thus could not be enslaved.

I want to be associated with a woman like that.

And with another straight person, from whom I never thought I'd hear support, someone also moved to take a radical step in response to this civil rights issue. It was more surprising coming from him, however, than from a white-haired judge with lots of mileage in South Africa; he's a toe-the-party-line Republican, the state legislator who represents our district and with whom I disagree on too many issues. Yet when he stood at the podium during the constitutional convention's long session on the "one man, one woman" marriage amendment, he spoke as though he were channeling God.

The previous hours of debate had been grueling—it was a civil rights issue, it wasn't; queers were good citizens, they weren't—with most of the speakers relying on well-crafted speeches and rhetorical flourishes that put considerable distance on the subject. But when Representative Sean Kelly stood up, he sounded purified, stripped clean. "What this is really about," he said slowly, as though every syllable took effort, "is love. That's what we're really discussing here—love." He named a colleague, a Democrat from Boston, someone he sat near during legislative sessions, and the tenderness in his voice made it clear that he loved her. And that he couldn't imagine denying her or her partner such basic rights as hospital access or the chance to stay in the home they owned together, should one of them die. When he said "love" it carried the weight of sacrament. It lofted above the suits and ties and mahogany and leather, above the microphones and whisperings and power brokering around him; it occupied a large space in the great chamber and then settled in our small room, and we cried in front of the television and knew he had gotten it just right.

I call to make a restaurant reservation, telling the young woman who answers the phone that we are a party of six, three lesbian couples who will have just married, and we would like one of the tables overlooking the river. "Sure," she says. "That's cool."

Her casual approach seems appropriate. I don't want special treatment. I don't want to give this day a glamorous frame; to do so suggests that I've longed for the moment when I, too, could marry, a feeling like that of the kid who never gets picked to be on a team, but sits on a bench until a coach or parent notices.

And, of course, I have.

"No toasters, just toasts," we repeat, and of course we are delighted by each gift that comes—plants, bouquets, champagne, cards, and an engagement cake covered with pansies and fresh fennel.

And when there is almost no time left to back out, my spouse-to-be remembers a story she once read, about an incident that took place in 1965, immediately after the Voting Rights Act was passed. The African American woman telling the story recalled a white man approaching her father to shake his hand and offer congratulations. "This is a great victory for your people," the white man said, to which her father replied, "Thank you, sir, but the victory is *yours*. It takes great courage to make amends." That's when I begin drafting the words I want to say before the justice of the peace pronounces us married, promises I will be glad to make in the presence of others, along the lines of loving and cherishing *for as long as I am able*. And then the sentence that makes the process more bearable. *And may the step we take today help make the world a more equitable place for all people.*

Reliance

I BACK THE TRACTOR out of the barn, get down on my hands and knees, and study the way the mower is attached. Two familiar messages sound equally loud in my head: *I can do this.* And: *Can I do this?* One of the blades had come off earlier in the week, when Holly was mowing, in a terrible grinding and strewing of metal parts. And now, though I'd rather be at the river or working in the garden, I kneel instead in gravel, remove the cotter pins, and free the bolts holding the main pulley in place. After dragging out the mower, I flip it over, a turtle on its back, missing one of its legs.

The other is badly bent, and both it and the one still attached are so dull and pitted it's hard to tell how the edges sliced grass. I take off the second blade and rue that I don't have an anvil or large vise. I make do with a maul and a concrete block, slamming the heavy hammer against the bent blade a few times. Then I push a block of wood into the shade for a stool, sit down with the blade clamped between my feet, and start filing, diagonal strokes toward the edge, black metal slow to yield silver. As sweat gathers on my back, I think how much easier it would be to borrow a truck, take the tractor to a repair shop, and let someone else deal with grease and scraped skin. But something insists that I do this myself, something that won't relax its hold on me, and while for the most part I like the independence it affords, it's a trait that has also gotten me into trouble more than once.

An hour or so later, the pieces back together, I start the tractor, engage the mower, and shift into gear. The tractor bucks and shudders, and I know I didn't reshape the blade quite right, but this time nothing flies off and I can see cut grass in my wake. I circle the lower field and head home for a beer.

"*Why* did you learn how to do that?" the horse whisperer asks. We're eating pieces of yellow sheet cake in a room full of prisoners and the best I can manage is a shrug. He deserved something better. We were, after all, the team that won at Chairs for Pairs, our arms linked together as we raced for a seat each time the music stopped. Elbow to elbow, we had had to find the right balance between caution and roughness—yank too hard and it might be misconstrued; don't yank hard enough and you might miss a chair. We kept from getting tangled in each other's legs and were the only ones left sitting when the game came to an end. But finding a better answer than "because I'm a lesbian" or "self-reliance is in my genes" requires too much explaining. I still haven't figured out why I chose to spend this particular weekend in prison with men convicted of violent crimes.

For several years, the Alternatives to Violence Project has been organized by a couple from our Quaker Meeting, who invite us to participate or become cofacilitators with the inmates who have finished their training. The time suddenly seemed right to join them, and now my role is similar to that of the twenty-odd prisoners—learning ways to take responsibility for the decisions we make, while creating a community that holds us up in adhering to those decisions. The main difference between all of us, at least for this long weekend, is that I get to go home at night. Like the men, I have much to surrender at the main entrance, including my driver's license and considerable autonomy; unlike them, I don't have to strip or get orifices checked, and the metal detector's sweep around my body is brief.

When the first session finally began—some of the men having waited months to participate in the program—we sat in a circle and learned about the games we would play, the exercises we would do, the times we would pair up or talk as a whole group. Then we were off at a pace that seemed edgy and fast, the inmates white and black and Hispanic, teenaged and white-haired, shy and vociferous, a few so eager to have an audience they forget how to stop talking. The setup allowed time for both earnestness and vulnerability, which seemed risky given what might happen when they returned to their cells at day's end, but which bound us fairly quickly in a sense of who we were as a unit.

We gave ourselves nicknames; we played Chairs for Pairs. And then the long-haired man who once robbed a Wells Fargo truck had us go around the circle and tell something about ourselves that made us proud.

"I'm a gourmet cook," said the first. "I have a three-year-old daughter," said the next, each becoming something different than a man in look-alike tan clothes. "I write gospel music." "I'm a *champeen* soccer player." The horse whisperer knew horses far better than people, and next to him was a Ping-Pong ace, leg-twitching and wiry. Then it was my turn. "I'm good at sheetrocking." My voice and hands described the room I had just finished remodeling, the skim coat so smooth you couldn't see a seam. Several men nodded and the focus moved on. "I'm a sharp dresser." "I started my own hair salon."

At last we broke for coffee, and one of the inmates rolled in the cart holding the first of the yellow cakes. It was then that the horse whisperer asked about my recent project, and I told him about knocking out a chimney, gutting four walls, and then adding new windows and bookshelves and trim. I didn't mention Holly or the fact that it was just the two of us in an old farmhouse together. On his face was the same surprise that had shown up on my mother's. "Where did you learn how to do all this?" she had asked, standing inside the new room, which made me realize how much we're still filling in from all those years we lived miles apart. But he put to me the question that she and I never mention: "*Why* did you learn how to do that?"

Driving home that night, leaving behind the clanging doors and endless loops of razor wire, I review their faces one by one and see men I could learn a lot from, if we had had more time to tell about our lives, men I could ask for help if they were on the outside and I were in trouble. I'm still surprised that I picked sheetrocking as my distinguishing trait rather than, say, having once hiked the length of the Appalachian Trail or having walked into an ice-covered pond to rescue a friend's dog that was trapped. Compared to the men in prison, I have thin bones, good

teeth, and few scars, and yet I wanted them to see me as
someone able to take care of herself, rather than someone
who carries around a sense of vulnerability.

I roll down the car window for the cold air that will
keep me awake once I leave the interstate and see Orion
perched just above the horizon. Something about the
constellation—solitary archer on a clear autumn night—
makes me wonder again about the balance we each find,
between relying solely on ourselves or depending on another, between rushing for our own chairs or getting
there with a companion. There's danger in taking either
position too far, as the men in prison made clear. Each
stepped over a line and was caught, as I almost did once,
though I recovered without paying too high a price. And
yet, I still toe the line; I can feel it. My participation in
AVP, which I thought was simply to learn more about it,
may actually be as instructive for me as for the inmates,
helping all of us recognize the line that separates a reckless, solo act from the place of making decisions with a
community in mind.

It's a relief to pull into the driveway and see the bedroom light still on.

Days later, we can't bear any more news of war or stay
inside another minute, and so we layer in thick clothes
and head for the ridge behind our house. Almost as soon
as we enter the woods, we hear a stick breaking under
something's foot. "Deer," I mouth to Holly, imagining
the one I sometimes see when working in the garden.
We hold still and listen for its progress. When the sound
crests the hill, we walk quietly on, watching for a flash
of white tail.

But it's a person who lifts up from behind a fallen log, and he's holding a gun and aiming at my chest. "Hey," I yell. "Hey!" He doesn't lower his arms. Two other men appear, also with guns and in camouflage, their faces covered by dark balaclavas. I hold out my hands to show they're empty. "We're just passing through," Holly says. He doesn't turn away and mumbles something instead, but the fabric across his mouth absorbs all the sound. "It's all right." I work to keep my voice calm. "See? We're leaving." I follow Holly back down the trail and relive the last time I turned away from men with guns, when I knew it was just a matter of time before I took a shot in the back.

I hadn't meant to be arrested, but there we were, a group of us from the nearby Seneca Women's Peace Camp, on a walking tour through Waterloo, New York, in the summer of 1983. We were learning about the planners of the first women's rights convention—Elizabeth Cady Stanton, Lucretia Mott, her sister, Martha Wright. "This is where Mott lived," the tour leader had pointed out. "And this is where they met to discuss their plans." Then we had to stop, in front of us a large crowd of angry veterans and their angrier girlfriends, waving flags, shouting insults, and blocking our access to the main bridge over the town's canal. They didn't want any Commie Pinko Dykes in their town; they didn't want us protesting war, challenging the life they knew, and while we sorted out what to do, the sheriff arrived with his bullhorn and announced that if we didn't move, we'd be responsible for inciting a riot. The crowd loved it. They could act badly because the blame would be on us, and, sure enough, when they moved in, we were the ones the police dragged away.

They held us first in the courtyard of a county jail, and then in an emptied room of an elementary school. Though larger-than-life Disney characters danced across the walls, the rest of the place translated as prison: wire in the windows, cots set up in rows, and men with guns and dogs, circling the building outside.

On the morning of the third day, the guard who usually stood at the door wasn't there, I couldn't see anyone outside, and, without really thinking, I climbed to an upper window and jumped out. Another woman did the same right behind me. We raced for the nearby woods and I braced for that shot, the noise first and then the hit that would slam me to the ground.

It didn't come.

"We have to walk," I said as we caught our breath behind a tree. "The only way we'll get out is if we walk like we live here." Which is what we did, all the way to the road, where none of the passing police cars slowed for us. And it's what we did later, when the sheriff held a press conference and announced that two women had gone missing. And though the nightmares continued for years afterward—shots and then I'm down, like what happened to the students killed at Kent State—ultimately, nothing ever came of it. Nothing.

But it's what I hold onto now as we head down the hill. Walk, don't run, and no one will get hurt.

We cross the brook and see more men hunkered behind hemlocks. We talk louder; we try for answers. A military exercise? Rehearsal for a SWAT team? Survivalists readying for the next assault on America?

"The terrorists are here," says Holly. "And they look just like us."

We're too angry to go inside and walk instead along the road, while the wind ices our hands and keeps us moving fast. On our return, we see the men again, this time by the neighbor's side door, where they look small and sheepish. And then, of course, we recognize two of them and know that though they're old enough to drive, only one is old enough to enlist. This was a game they were playing, and we had stumbled into the middle of it.

We're as embarrassed as they are, hating the fact that toy guns had scared us, though with the news so full of war—Iraq, Afghanistan—it's hard not to think otherwise.

And then there's their mom, who calls to apologize. "Paintball," she says. "They didn't mean to scare you. In fact, if they'd known you might go walking, they would certainly have warned you." Her voice reconnects us. Her voice makes clear that none of us are in this alone, that though we might seesaw away from each other, we almost always find a way to come back, and I remember a time last spring when I couldn't figure out why my chainsaw kept stalling, and I was frustrated and tired of yanking the cord. Then I saw her husband's truck as he returned home from work, and I hurried over to see him, meeting where we often did to talk about teenagers and wildlife and two-cycle engines.

He nodded and took the saw, pulled the cord, and messed with the choke, and then he handed it back as it purred, his voice full of reassurance. "Try it like this," he said. "Keep the choke pulled halfway out," which I did and it's been running fine ever since, whether limbing pines, cutting brush, or keeping clear the path between us.

How to
Become a Generalist

1.

Get a job picking apples. Learn how to caress and three-in-hand them, travel limbs and ladders after them, and reach through wasps and branches until your bucket is full of them. Practice emptying your load into the fifteen-bushel bin until you're sure you're not the one bruising fruit. Take in the smell of hay and sweat and dry leaves. Let the tractor sounds surround you, and the calls of migrating geese. With your crewmates, swap tales and songs and silence, hour after hour, day after day, as autumn falls around you, the hills turn red and gold, and the sky stretches wide enough to admit no space to worry about pesticides and twig jabs and dew-slick ladders. Peel the apples before eating them. Love them. Dream them.

2.

Accept that some things have to come first, like safe homes and day-care centers and campaigns to stop ads that show chained women and roughed-up women and women pointing hair dryers shaped like guns at their heads, and, while you're at it, work to end war and the stockpiling of nuclear weapons and the military-industrial complex that's overtaking sovereign countries. Find jobs that help pay the bills, the kind with flexible hours just in case outrage gets the better of you and civil disobedience nets you some jail time. Keep in mind the line from the Charlie King song: "Your life is more than your work, and your work is more than your job."

Cut and bundle Christmas trees. Learn basic book-keeping. Hire out with the carpentry tools you've already come to use. Become an inventory specialist where, at night, you walk the long aisles of department stores, counting items on each shelf, across and back, up and down, your fingers tapping out formulas on the calculator attached to your hip. Pray you don't have to spend much time in the dairy section, which will chill you to the bone. Try not to notice the escaped parakeets, winging between ceiling beams, or the number of fish in the aquariums, floating belly-up.

3.

When the work or the arrests begin to wear you down, move to an island. Take a morning job at a boat shop, helping caulk and paint skiffs, then spend a few hours on land that you're helping clear, felling pines three times your age and wider than your arms stretched out twice. When too exhausted to start the chainsaw one more time, wander through the woods to the wigwam that you rigged next to a quiet saltwater pond, and try to sleep, though gulls and kids are still at play in the late-day light. At 10:00 p.m., feel your way back through the dark, rinse your body in the cold stream, and make coffee on the small gas stove. Then drive to the summer crafts school where you're paid to be the responsible person through the night, in and out of studios where artists shape new work.

When winter comes, carve spruce burls into bowls and sell them at craft fairs, and when a friend dies, a woman you helped tend throughout her final year, agree to help her son build a coffin. Measure her body carefully so the box fits just right and design it so nothing interferes with the slide that will mark the end of her long life.

4.

Remember what you learned when fasting in jail—how dust motes glinted in the light through a high window, and how the place inside you that chose not to eat felt like sinews and then like steel. Remember how vivid were your dreams and how real the sense of floating, meadows below that you knew and vaguely familiar rivers.

Let the daily cycle of tides soften the memories, the way it did your abraded body, from the time you flew off a speeding go-cart, your brother at the wheel, and the only thing slowing your flight was the drag of bare legs. Recall the many days you spent walking in the cold sting of ocean and then sitting splay-legged in the sun until the scabs had dried. Remember the new skin that emerged from all that itch and ache.

5.

Return, sturdier, to the mainland. Find a place where you know the land's stories. Learn about previous occupants who were drawn to the streams and south-facing slopes—the weavers and loggers, stonemasons and farmers, artists and anglers and entrepreneurs. Figure out what they did and do—lavender growing, candle making, glass blowing, coffee roasting—as you continue to teeter between a career and seasonal work. Pay little attention when your grandmother worries for those she calls "jacks-of-all-trades and masters of none." In the time you have to wander, think again about Margaret Fuller, writing in the 1850s, who lamented the limited scope of work for women and girls, some of whom, she pointed out, "like to saw wood, others to use carpenters' tools," and when "these tastes are indulged, cheerfulness and good-humor are promoted. Where they are forbidden, because 'such things are not proper for girls,' they grow sullen and mischievous."

6.

Admit your grandmother had a point, that doing one thing well has its merits. Study for the necessary degree, and begin finding your way in the classroom. When you visit her, swap stories about students, as she, too, was once a teacher, until she married your grandfather, after which no school district could hire her.

7.

Listen to those who say, "You can do it," like the grand-father who could fix or design anything—or so the older folks said, just as they said of his mother, who was *put out to work* at age six, and who could see a dress in a dress-maker's window and go home and make the same thing. Remember that he once spent a year in a TB ward, after having a lung cut out and several ribs removed (the cruelest thing, your grandmother will later say, she'd ever known a human to endure), and how care-ful he was with his breath, and how many times he sent you or one of your brothers, age eight, ten, twelve, up two-story ladders to clean windows or change lightbulbs, wasps all around and a view as far as the Isles of Shoals. Recall, too, all those times he gave you a clam fork and bucket and half an hour to dig sea worms, or sent you to drag in the dinghy before a fast-approaching storm, and how, after you left home for good, he was the one who bought you some of your first tools and gave you lessons in plumbing and wiring.

Hold all that in mind so that, right after he dies and a storm takes down wires all over the county, you can climb a ladder to splice in the phone line because the crews won't make it for days and you need to talk to your family. Then, at his funeral, tell about the time he sent you to the far sandbars, the ones that appeared only once a season, to get the sea clams he was craving. Describe how you were just tall enough to keep your head above water while feeling the clams with your feet, and how your sack was almost full when the clam warden caught you. Enjoy again how you stood your ground, your grandfather laughing from the cottage window, as you dumped your illegal catch and took the rap all by yourself.

8.

Buy a one-hundred-year-old farmhouse that includes land where you can grow food for much of the year. Put jacks under the sagging floor joists. Take out enough walls so the rooms aren't little and dark, and then insulate those that remain. Dig a garden as big as you can manage and prune the berry canes and rangy apple trees. Find the job that connects you with students and learn the local stories.

And now and again, on a clear summer day, lie outside in the grass, while the house settles, vegetables grow, and flowers rotate their blossoms toward the light. When a deer feeds ten feet away on new raspberry leaves, let it. Breathe the air it breathes. Sense its heft and wild power. Then feel the ways you have become part of the land and how the land now holds part of you, and in that moment, under that sky, let that be enough.

Companions

ON THE WINDOWSILL: A clutch of parsley inside a blue jar, and a caterpillar eating its way through the deeply ruffled leaves. Not on the sill: a net or cloth to hold this soon-to-be tiger swallowtail in this small area; it stays because of the food that's continually replaced.

I harvest more parsley in the cool of the morning, after picking peas for our supper and lettuce that the deer haven't sampled. The caterpillar humps backward when I insert more stems, then resumes its methodical chewing, growing fatter each day in the quiet of our kitchen.

Watching it eat, I feel companionable, as when the cat brushes my leg, a spider stretches in the bedroom, or a praying mantis raises her head, as did the one that shared the deck with us the year Holly and I lived in DC.

We had taken a shared job with the American Friends Service Committee, not far from Dupont Circle, in a house where the previous tenants had kept dozens of potted flowers on the deck. The half-barrel of blue iris drew the mantis in, and I learned to look for her each morning, though it often took several minutes to make out the green of her body against leaves of the same color, her forelegs cocked above a fattening abdomen. I wanted to watch her deliver the egg case she was nourishing, a frothy sack that would stiffen and turn brown and last through the winter, like the one that had hatched in my desk in fifth grade, spilling young into our class-room while we were off on a field trip. We returned to a stream of tiny mantises, heading for the walls and win-dows, and the transformation of our sturdy teacher into someone who could panic. She insisted we throw the egg case out the window and kill every one we saw. Though later, Sheri Beauchesne, who lived near enough to walk to school, grabbed the egg case on her way home along with the last of the hatchlings, while I had to wait in line for the bus, still stunned at the extent of the massacre. Fortunately, it wasn't a total loss: We saw a few the next day on the ceiling and some on the cafeteria walls, and all of them so high we could do nothing but point and laugh and avoid our teacher's eyes.

What I have never seen, however, is the way a fe-male eats the male, after—and sometimes during, as the nineteenth-century scientist Jean-Henri Fabre once described it—the lengthy act of mating. "Oh what sav-agery!" he writes. "She practices the equivalent of can-nibalism, that hideous peculiarity of man." He watched a male hold a female "in a tight embrace. But the wretch has no head; he had no neck; he has hardly a body. The other, with her muzzle turned over her shoulder, con-tinues very placidly to gnaw what remains of the gentle swain. And all the time, that masculine stump, holding on firmly, goes on with the business!"

The act takes self-sacrifice for the sake of the kids to a new extreme, but it was not a practice I was likely to see in DC, the mantis on the deck already impregnated and alone and fairly lethargic through the heat of that long fall.

I began to watch out for her and saw her more regularly than I did any of the other neighbors, surrounded as we were by offices and embassies and fast-moving businesspeople, and if it weren't for my two coworkers, a woman from Eritrea, another from Ethiopia, the mantis might have begun to approximate a friend. I loved that she was in the city, just a few blocks from a busy intersection, and that no one else seemed to know she was there.

Then we moved and I missed her briefly, probably more than I'll miss this swallowtail when it transforms its package of body parts and eventually flies off. But I'll remember each for a peculiar kind of company, like a chance encounter with a stranger, who wants nothing more than to be near a warm body in the bus station or share a drink in the dusky light of a bar.

Deciphering Bird

FROM A DISTANCE THEY sounded like a storm or train, a rumbling that then separated into millions of wings. The sky darkened as they passed, the heavy commotion a pressing weight, a noisy, dusty covering that kept coming and coming. And when at last they moved on and light spread again over the earth, the quiet seemed both obvious and odd—until they settled for the night in a nearby stand of oak, and an occasional branch gave way under the weight of two or three hundred or more birds.

A century later the birds' story still feels biblical, theirs a collective force that was the next test—like grasshoppers, the plague, the next sky-borne threat that only another Job could endure. In fact, the birds had become the experiment, the smallest of Jobs, suffering such afflictions that could only be explained as another deal God had plotted with Satan.

Explosions will knock you from the trees at night, hands will break your flock-mates' necks, and everywhere will be the smell of blood and spent shot. In the thrash of warm

bodies and those already cold, you will find that no place is safe, that wherever you try to light, someone will want to eat you, and when you take to the sky, you will never know who will plummet next from the flock.

Soon you will lose night in addition to day, for in your exhausted state you will be asleep when the hunters come at dawn along with the quick-fingered boys carrying wooden bats and burlap bags. Then you will lose the comfort of the flock, the familiarity of birds on every side, birds that look just like you, that help you bank and stay aloft and find your way and locate food, a single fluid organism made up of thousands of your kin, each of you cross-shaped in flight. Yet soon your numbers will be reduced to a ragged, restless thousand, staggering along the old routes, never knowing if that glint of metal below means a nearby farm and peace and food or the sun on a gun aiming now at you.

Having lost most points of reference, you will quickly lose your bearings and your senses will soon seem like someone else's. No wall of bird scent will surround you, and the hidden perch you sometimes find won't feel quite right, no family members pressed against your shoulders, no rowdy crowding to reassure you before sleep. In your solitary flight, you won't even recognize the new feeling of breeze, bereft of all those bodies that helped with shear and shelter from the wind. You will lose all sense of cohesion. You will cry out for an answer but will hear none, nor will your friends gather and quarrel with you over whether or not you have sinned, as they, too, are desperate for a break from the killing.

In the hours empty of guns, you will hear trains and the new and noisy cars and birds that never meant much to you—the banging of a grouse, the chatter of a wren,

*the repertoire of mockingbirds that accentuate your alone-
ness. As you flutter about in confusion, you will miss the
old ways, your muscles grown thin with your hunger.*

*And then, when you think you've reached the bottom
of your despair, that the jig must be up and someone will
intervene at last and stopper the guns, force down the nets
and sour your flavor so the cooks will overlook you; when
you are sure that old Beelzebub must finally admit that
God has won yet again, as there are, after all, but ten of
you left on the planet and thus the time has come to hear
that voice from above—*Stop. Enough. O pathetic ones,
you have served me well and fattened your fellow creatures and taught them about plenty, which they thought
meant excess, and all the while you never tried to live
above your station—*you will be sorely disappointed.*

*For there is no voice, no thunder, no parting of the heav-
ens, and the last of you will die in solitary confinement.*

I wish I had heard it, the motion of a million passenger pigeons, like rain but not falling to land. I would
have tilted back my head, closed my eyes and felt *Bird,*
solely *Bird,* quick-winged T's all about me, with their
thin bones and pink chests and small heads.

I wish I had heard the other extinct ones, too—the
boom of the heath hen, and the Carolina parakeet's
squawk, or seen the great auk, with its big feet and
small wings, a perfect shape for distance swimming, and
clumsy and trusting when approached by sailors on land.

I have heard the ivory-billed woodpecker's cry, but it
was a taped recording, played inside a house, and nothing about it said *Swamp* or *Survivor* or *Large Black Bird
with White Bill.*

If our timing and location proves right, however, one of us just might see the last of another fast-declining bird, the red knots—chunky gray shorebirds that turn chestnut for mating season. It would do us all good to watch them come down to the shore in vast numbers and start skittering along the beach, a shimmering carpet of red birds, in their few days of rest and furious feeding after thousands of miles of nonstop travel. But if we're late or misjudge the winds, the window will close, and soon they, too, will be gone, erased from two continents and a broad swath of sky.

My body listens at night; I cannot stop its hearing—the hum of the house, the bang of pipes, the floors that heave and settle. It takes longer to sort out a fainter sound, though it's not clear how I hear it: the late-summer pull of migrating birds, thousands and thousands of bodies passing overhead, too high for their calls to reach our ears, for us to know they're in motion, unless, using telescopes, we see them pass in front of the full moon or note the dark clouds on weather radar that have nothing to do with storms.

Though I've spent my whole life deciphering *Bird*, taking in their calls the way some people do human tunes— the crows announcing an owl, the flickers a hawk, or the blue jays a hunter slipping through the thick scrub—all I sense from the knots is *the journey*, which seems to have run into trouble, which means sleep for me is becoming more difficult.

Their labor starts near the Arctic Circle, above Hudson Bay—the adults' courtship, egg laying, and training of chicks taking place within two hectic months.

Then they all head south, over half of them barely six weeks old, the first stop a thousand miles away—Massachusetts for some, for others, Delaware Bay. There they stoke up on food—mussel spat, small coquinas packing on fat before becoming airborne again, flying as high as fifteen thousand feet, the shoulder of South America their next destination.

It's a miracle of design, of navigational ability, tiny birds traveling between forty and fifty miles per hour without having to refuel, without having to rehydrate, and without ceasing their wing strokes for a full five days and nights. They set down in southern Brazil; they eat and sleep and eat some more, then they hie off to Patagonia, where it's summer and easy, and there's plenty to eat for a few months of relative quiet before their cells tell them it's time to make the long journey all over again.

In their wake is a mystery of considerable proportion. Though they spend much of their lives focused on the ground right in front of them, somehow they figured out the bigger picture—that summer exists at opposite times of the year at the farthest ends of the hemisphere. What did the original birds smell or learn from the stars? Was it the way the earth rotates or the continents' shift that sent them into the air, flying nine thousand miles to reach a second home? Who led the way? And when did it first happen that small knots flew five days without stopping?

They are the birds I want to see soon, though the numbers make clear that they're on a fast arc to extinction. Ten years may be all they have left, and we as slow as great auks in our response to this news.

How I hate the story of Job! How I lament the paucity of translators for the language of *Bird*. How hard that the loudest voice is the one I resist hearing.

You, who have been so good and steady—so able in your feats of risk and flight—shall find yourselves in an exhausted state with no place on land to settle. The beaches will be full of dogs and trucks and kids flying kites, so that each time you near shore, a racing beast or ATV will force you back into the air. Your hunger will daunt you but you will not be permitted to eat. Even in the rocky coves, where people and their pets seldom venture, the usual sources of food won't be found, as the ocean will have become too warm, mussels and clams unable to breed in the newly tepid waters.

And though you try to time your arrival with that of the horseshoe crabs, those ancient beings whose life cycle you evolved to meet, they will no longer be dragging their humped bodies onto sand, mating and shedding eggs that number in the millions. You can wait a full week—fasting the whole while—but they won't show up, for they, too, are on the list—killed for bait, for fertilizer, for their valuable blood, or simply because they feed on the clams that people want, and they have a dangerous sharp spine and are so easy to flatten. And with no horseshoe crab eggs to eat, your cells will stay thin, your muscles limp, and it will be harder to move your wings in the rhythm you once knew.

You will lose your bearings and all sense of unity, your flockmates dead, your sense of lift and sheer thrown off. You will cry out but it won't matter, for it will happen that soon, that the last of you will tip over and you will all be gone.

Interventions

OF ALL THE IMAGES, the hardest one to shake is of a man falling headfirst, past floor after floor of the soon-to-collapse building. Over six thousand people missing and feared dead—more than all the kids at the bus stops, old folks in nursing homes, day laborers and artists and shopkeepers in my town of Buckland, more, in fact, than in the towns of Buckland and Shelburne and Colrain combined—and I find myself in need of a century-long perspective.

Inside my grandmother's living room, it is still and warm, and so is she, and small on the couch and glad to see me. I lean down for a press of cheek and careful hug, and then settle in, close to her good ear. She knows what I want to talk about and tells me what she feels.

"We should exercise restraint," she says, "and plenty of patience," and I feel safer than I have since the moment a delivery man told me I should turn on the news because the United States was being hijacked.

She sees no need for a punitive military strike, and she shudders at such phrases as "dead or alive" and "we'll smoke them out of their caves." Hers is the long view, shaped by hard times and a strong will, having survived the 1918 influenza, which affected one in every four Americans, and the temporary loss of her husband twenty years later, when he spent a year in a TB ward and a subsequent year in silence, having been told that if he spoke the growths in his throat might metastasize and kill him. She lived through the Great War and the terrible ones that followed and has seen how hatred becomes enflamed and as easily fades within short decades. She knows the divisiveness of yellow ribbons, the dangerous uses of the flag, and the importance of the freedom to stand up and disagree. She has also watched far more TV news these last few days than is her custom, and she has returned from despair once again, her warmth making possible a belief in tomorrow.

She soon steers the talk to her interest in the students at the nearby college where I teach, and I relax into the spill of afternoon sun through the wall of south-facing windows. It is all so welcome that I don't take my usual care with answers nor feel wary of hers; today I want to tell her everything, from the politics of the English Department to the responsibilities I feel for my lover's grown children.

But then there's a bird at the feeder, and she needs to know what it is. She leans forward a few inches, forcing focus from eyes that weep and itch and complicate reading and writing. She makes out what she can of the bird's outline, its color and size, the aggressive way it feeds, and then she leans back with a nod. "A female rose-breasted grosbeak. One of a pair that's been coming all summer."

Pleased, she again tilts her face toward me, though I can tell her eyes haven't readjusted to the closeness. It doesn't matter. Nor does it matter that I know she has seen thousands of such grosbeaks in her life, since growing up on a farm in Maine, where she learned about the birds that interested her father, and then organizing a life that included regular study of them. It's unlikely she'll ever add another species to her life list, but each bird at the feeder poses a test of her skills. In that brief moment, everything else has to wait, even the talk of war and what it might mean to the nation. A bird at the feeder is a test of her faculties, a chance to prove her mind still works the ways she needs it to.

I, too, leave behind the images of blown-out ambulances, of fleeing, ash-covered people, a huge fist of grit and rubble bulging behind them. We hover instead inside the comfort of cardinals and chickadees, woodpeckers and nuthatches, all brisk and busy as schoolkids at recess.

When it comes time to leave, she doesn't want me to go, though we both know this will never be easy. I can't patch the hole left when her husband of seventy years died, nor speed up the process of learning to live alone. And she can't fully engage me in describing the life I now lead, the home she hasn't seen, the lifestyle she won't ask about. We cling but a moment and I promise to return soon.

As I drive west into the hills, passing fields where bear and raccoon raid the corn in the summer, deer and turkey wander in the winter, and coyotes hunt the edges as vultures drift overhead, the sense of a tamed and warm world begins to fade. The radio news includes updates on the achingly small number of bodies found in the rubble, and, against the tattoo of a pending war, I struggle with how little we know about the effects we have on the world, let alone on these few square miles. The delicate balance of relationships seems far too easy to disrupt.

In the weeks that follow, people seem careful and glad with each other, lingering over coffee and sidewalk talk. Cars move slower on the road; more drivers wave as they pass. At the monthly planning board meeting, no one is in a hurry to leave after our business is over, as though we can't bear to rush away from each other's company. Everywhere in town there is talk of vigils and local protests, while tenderness for each other is what comes through the loudest. As though we know we've been spared the worst and now can't take any life or love for granted.

From the kitchen stoop, I watch a cardinal fly through the line of hemlocks and down to the brook, where it drinks and bathes. Juncos feed under the blackberry canes while a pair of chickadees inspects branches above them. I don't know if the birds are here because a bird-feeder used to be nearby or if this would be a haunt anyway. For a moment it's tempting to retrieve the feeder that I dismantled when we moved in, its wide bottom and open sides too much of an invitation to bears. I could put it or another in the same spot, which we could see from the kitchen, the cardinal's unlikely red appearing as a regular surprise in our days.

Though if the red birds' numbers continue rising as fast as they have the last few decades, we might also cease noticing, the way I hardly care about the intense blue of the jays, for we have always had them with us; the cardinal, however, is still in the process of spreading north, its way smoothed by milder winters and the prevalence of feeders. A hundred years ago, a cardinal seen in the winter anywhere in the Northeast was probably an escapee from somebody's house. Before the 1918 Migratory Bird

Treaty banned the buying and selling of songbirds, the sale of cardinals was a predictable and lucrative business. A home was a lovelier place, many people believed, if it included at least one red bird in a cage.

But other birds would come as well, and I remember the feeders my mother kept when I was little, and the first time chickadees fed from my hand. A friend and I had discovered that, if the feeders were empty, small birds were willing to take seeds from our palms. Soon we lured them to the tops of our heads, even our cheeks, for the prick of tiny claws on our skin and the danger of thin bills near our eyes.

The scolding notes of a dozen birds signals a cat in the yard, one of a half dozen that visit this land. The neighborhood seems to have more pets than kids, the animals healthy and well fed and happier to be outside than in. But it's cats rather than dogs that do the damage, joining those across North America that kill an estimated billion birds each year.

My feeder idea vanishes. I want the local birds to be leery of our homes and our intentions, aware that we're unpredictable, and that we're not doing them any favors when we seduce them to feeders that we might or might not keep filled all winter.

Our nation has begun its twin-pronged response to Afghanistan. The first planes drop bombs, and the next scatter food aid. Packages from the latter contain enough calories for a day, a meatless meal costing about $3.95. The former carries thousand-pound warheads that can wipe out factories and homes and airplanes, at an average cost of about $1 million. Twenty years ago the United

States spent over a billion dollars training and arming anti-Soviet forces in the region we're now bombing, making it the country's largest covert operation since Vietnam. Those earlier weapons and well-trained men are now of considerable concern, another consequence of a policy that was terribly shortsighted. But that's not what's making the news or what my brother wants to hear in the evening when he calls.

"What would you have us do?" he asks. "If someone in the family takes a hit, you're not going to sit back and do nothing, are you?" I would prefer to lean against him rather than talk on the phone, enjoying his easy power and the way he wells up when talking about his kids. Instead I remind him about the premises we abide by in this country, that it's not OK to kill because there's been killing, to destroy because there's been destruction. We have courts; we have laws; we're not a nation of assassins. But I stop when I hear the anguish in his voice about the possible response of his sons and whether they will feel they have to take up arms, and he's scared and wants them safe. And of course I want that, too.

In the village, colored leaves float above the reflection of gold hills and a sky that changes colors as clouds shift past in the wind. I watch from the bridge as sparrows slip in and out of the abutments, their distinct chatter rising above the steady churn of water. And then, as though I can't escape more reminders of lives out of balance, all I see is more evidence of interventions that didn't go well.

The sparrows were brought here, from England in the 1850s, to protect city trees from the cankerworms that were devouring their leaves. The birds did the job so well that more were imported, though soon it became clear that they preferred grain over insects, and they found plenty of it in the horse droppings that littered the cities. As the sparrow's numbers exploded, its bad habits became more obvious—"thief, wretch, feathered rat . . . injurious, pernicious, disreputable, salacious, quarrelsome and even murderous," according to Edward Forbush, Massachusetts' state ornithologist. They decimated crops; they raided grain stores, and they drove out other birds that kept insects at bay. "The only one of the smaller birds," Forbush writes, "that has repeatedly been seen to destroy the nests of other birds, break their eggs, kill their young, mob them, and drive them away from their homes."

In most North American cities, English sparrows are still the most common bird, though it's a smaller number today than at its peak a century ago, when birds rushed by the hundreds for a puddle, a crust of bread, a spill of horse grain. In places like New York City, starving kids were doing the same thing. The response to the desperate children, however, was to ship them on orphan trains to points far west of the city, an idea that seemed noble at the time, though the kids typically had no idea where they were going or why or for how long. The Children's Aid Society, founded by Charles Loring Brace, simply dressed them in clean clothes and sent them forth to parade at train platforms, with the hope that a kind family would take them in—one hundred thousand kids distributed over seventy-five years. In the end, the man who had put the plan into motion wasn't quite sure it was worth the cost. "When a child of the streets stands before you, in rags, with a tear-stained face, you cannot easily forget him," said Brace. "And yet, you are perplexed what to do.

The human soul is difficult to interfere with. You hesitate how far you should go."

The sparrows, meanwhile, were poisoned or shot, bounties offered in some cities for boxes of bodies. But the carnage hardly slowed them; it was the car that finally did. When urban horses gave way to gas-powered vehicles, the birds' main source of food disappeared and the sparrows died by the thousands. But the ordeal wasn't over for those that survived, for in came another bird species that outhustled them to food.

The house finch, like the English sparrow, is also tied to human activity, in its case the nationwide rise in bird feeders. The few birds released on Long Island in 1941 liked living close to people, and, with their cheery song and rosy head and breast, most people liked them back. But within a few decades, there were too many of them, and they were too aggressive, meaning they crowded the feeder perches, ate their fill of seed, and chased off the more reticent species. But before birders opted to adopt some of the same tactics used with English sparrows (such as drowning or suffocating those that oust bluebirds from nesting boxes), house finches began showing up with red and runny eyes, sometimes so encrusted the birds can't open them. It's a conjunctivitis that can blind them, caused by bacteria that spread at feeding stations.

"Bird feeding is killing birds," writes Eirik A. T. Blom in an issue of *Bird Watcher's Digest* that I find at my grandmother's, and feeding them, he suggests, "may have been killing birds for a long time." He writes of purple finches and pine siskins that have been dying at feeders throughout the country, also doves in the Southwest, and hawks that prey on them. "Redpolls in

Alaska. Quail in the Southwest . . . These are no longer
isolated or anecdotal events, and new instances are crop-
ping up weekly."

Blom wants to eliminate the whole bird-feeding practice, though with an estimated thirty million households
in the United States with bird feeders and billions of dollars invested annually in maintaining them, it's become
a habit that's unlikely to change any time soon.

The reason is simple: The decision to feed birds has
little to do with the cost or the threat of disease or the
hassle of keeping feeders clean and filled. It's about having a tiny life force appear right outside the window, providing an intimate moment of contact that helps keep
loneliness at bay. And what makes it even simpler is that
birds are wild and arrive of their own volition, and their
shapes are nonthreatening and their markings seem
perfect, and they stitch us into a network that stretches
around the world.

A month after the 9/11 bombings, the president addresses the nation, updating us on America's war against
terrorism. He is firm and positive—we have rallied, he
says, we will prevail; we will not stop until terrorism is
uprooted from the world, until governments have been
held accountable for the thugs they feed and shelter. He
is vague in places, but cheerfully so, in terms of what
such a policy might mean for countries like Syria and
Iraq; he sounds strong and buoyant about the United Na-
tions' role in helping shape a new Afghanistan. He is op-
timistic even when relaying the FBI's warning about the
newest threat to the country. We have reason to believe,
the president says, that another strike could occur on

U.S. soil in the next few days, and he's sorry he can't tell us more than that. Americans, he says, should go about their daily business as much as possible. And the best way to do that, he says, is to *shop.*

I turn off the news, shuddering at such advice. To my way of thinking, honing an appetite for more shoes, more cars, more oil, or more land, will only keep us in the position of *wanting,* forever in pursuit of goods whether we need them or not, a strategy guaranteed to keep us from ever feeling sated. I see us going forth like small Pac-Mans, all mouth and no legs, eating our way around the globe as we bounce from want to want and place to place. I wish to hear someone with the clarity of John Woolman, a Quaker who took to towns and meetinghouses in the mid-eighteenth century, pointing out that most conflicts are rooted in our appetite for owning things. The ownership he specifically addressed involved the keeping of slaves, and it troubled him terribly that fellow Quakers, who believe that there is that of God in everyone, were not seeing Him in the Africans they were buying and selling. Woolman launched a campaign of far-reaching reform, with a clear and simple message at the heart of it. "Look to thy possessions," he said, "for in them you will find the seeds of war."

The sound in the woods is like that of rain, though the sun is shining and there are no clouds in the sky. It's the fall of autumn's abundance, leaves and seeds and needles that chatter against branches as they scrape their way down. Acorns bounce when they hit, as do butternuts and pinecones, and nowhere is it quiet for long. In a momentary lull, I hear the high calls of brown creepers and kinglets, small birds that I will love even more in a sun-lit clearing in January, delicate creatures that will never be lured to bird feeders. I wish all my interactions with birds were this simple and unmediated, as random as the time a chickadee landed on my sock when I was out hiking and began filling its bill with bits of wool.

As I scuff home through fallen leaves, I think of Nigsti, the woman from Eritrea with whom Holly and I worked in DC, and the only person I've ever met who was unfazed by American goods. She immigrated with her youngest child to escape her country's deadly skirmishes with Ethiopia, planning to stay only long enough for the war to be resolved and her daughter to graduate from college. A faithful member of the Christian Coptic Church, she fasted on holy days, shared *injera* when she was eating, and was never tempted by the fads that seemed to sweep up other immigrants.

When she learned that Holly and I would soon be leaving the city, she announced an afternoon party, which would also include our coworker Sara, originally from Ethiopia, who helped with translations from Amharic to English. On a cold December day, Nigsti roasted green coffee beans over the gas stove in the kitchen before moving us to the enclosed porch, where she made coffee and a large batch of popcorn over a small charcoal burner. Incense wafted around us, and the windows dimmed with fog. Huddled close for warmth, we reused the words we had in common, mimed what we couldn't say, and preferred to laugh through some of the confusion than have Sara set us straight. In between, we sipped strong coffee, let silence soften the afternoon's edges, and loved Nigsti as daughters would, though she was only a few years older. But her tattoos and facial scars and experience with war had aged her in a way we hadn't yet known.

When I'm almost to the house, I stop and fill my pockets with chestnuts, surprised that the squirrels have gathered so few this year. I finger their sleek skins, not quite sure why Nigsti drifted into my thoughts when she did, and then see her as the reminder of an uncompromised life, and as an example of a way to resist the calls to excess and more violence.

A flock of Canada geese flies noisily overhead, handsome and triumphant and in higher numbers than last year, and for now it doesn't matter that I know their whole story—that they have become obstacles for nearby golfers and have fouled local waters and have grown fat and happy on the corn people put out for them. Against this late afternoon sky, they're simply a joy to hear and see, and I watch until they're long gone from sight.

Catch and Release

THERE WAS NEVER ANY accounting for the things that appealed to thieves after they broke open the door on the seldom-traveled dirt road. One year, they backed up a truck and took the cabin's entire contents—chests, beds, the kitchen table and chairs. Another year, all the smaller things went—kerosene lamps, plates, cups, pans. But this recent break-in was for the woodstove, yanked fast enough from the pipe that a cloud of ash billowed through the room. And then someone grabbed the fish off the wall on his way out, taking the only evidence of our father's prowess with a fly rod, caught when he was still in his teens. The other records of memorable fish— big, small, beautiful, numerous—were written in pencil between studs on the cabin wall, mostly in our grand-father's quick scrawl. They, too, are now gone, covered over with insulation and pine boards, where no one is likely ever to read them again.

His few oil paintings still hang there, as do the joke plaques we six siblings loved as kids—the angler's prayer ("to catch a fish so big that even I, when talking of it afterwards may never need to lie"), the warning to tres-passers (of a "double barrel shotgun that ain't loaded

101

with sofa pillers"), and the description of a fisherman ("and when the day is far spent he returneth, smelling of strong drink and the truth is not in him"). The bawdy lines had nothing to do with our parents' sensibilities and probably less to do with our grandfather's, but they stayed on the cabin's walls because he had put them there. He did the same with the splendid trout that his only child had caught, packing it immediately on ice and then hurrying over rough roads to deliver it to a taxidermist. In its place there's now but an oval shadow, with no trace of the golden color of both fish and mount—a five-pound rainbow trout, seventeen inches long, with enough curve and heft to suggest the power it once possessed. A quick flip of its tail and it would be gone, a dark flash across our dreams in the bedroom where we slept.

Fishing occupied that kind of space inside of our grandfather, though not so in our dad, who put his rod away forever after the day he was out in a canoe and his cast embedded a hook in his middle son's cheek (even though the rest of us remember the joy of the night afterward, all of us in the car for the long drive on narrow roads to take Arthur to the doctor, and then the dozens of deer we saw in the car headlights on the narrow roads back to the cabin). It's my grandfather, then, who accompanies me when I enter the river, forty years after he died and thirty years after I last messed about with his rod. It was a surprise to have him show up, though it was also a surprise that I wanted a fishing license, and suddenly decided to stop on my way past the town clerk's office. She didn't act as though it were out of the ordinary, though I had never paid for such a license before. But I wasn't quite sure what else to do, given the story I had just heard from my father.

I bought a rod and several dozen flies; I studied the river; I found good access points near deep pools and long riffles. And now he's with me with each arc of arm, each spin of reel and flare of line. I don't know what he would make of my choice of flies—*Coachman, Blue-Winged Olive, Light Cahill*—and I doubt he ever fished this particular river. Still, I like his company and the rattle of a kingfisher and the furl of mist around a dark curve just upstream. Then a fish hits my fly and I can think of nothing else but that I'm connected to a living being that I can't even see.

The line mimes the action—fight, pause, flee; a moment of slack and it's almost over, a fast dash and it's clear we're still bound together, the pole vibrating with fish energy, fish resistance, fish will. Another crossing of the river and another, and then he slows and almost as slowly I reel him in, not sure I want to see what felt so fierce and large a force.

How pale he is in contrast to the one caught in mid-swim on the cabin wall! And how thin—barely a third of Dad's prize fish in its weight. I keep it long enough to admire its sheen and speckling and hard slap against my hand, and then let it go, a narrow bulge of water marking its fast run downriver.

Its new wariness will make it tougher for the next angler to catch, and I wonder if my grandfather ever fished from a bank like this or stepped into a river in chest-high waders. In film footage my father shot when still a boy, and in the mental photographs I carry of him, he is in a canoe or small rowboat, fishing lakes in Maine or Vermont, with room on either side to cast; I never saw him balancing on slick rocks, inspecting the newest crop of insects rising from the surface. Yet as I wade toward

another pool, it becomes clear that he is the reason I re-
learned how to tie a fly and feed line into the cast, years
after his tackle was dispersed to other family members.
Whatever it was that fishing came to mean in his life will
mean more to me now, because first there was the fire
and then the solace of open water and the cure to which
he kept returning as long as he was able.

He was but a kid when it happened, busy in a kid's
rushing way, when he knocked over a lamp, and that's
all it took, one moment of hurry, a lit lamp breaking on
the floor, and enough kerosene to send the house and all
its contents up in flames—food, furniture, clothes, photos, the precious upright piano. The family, reluctant to
accept help when too few had anything extra, struggled
through the subsequent lean years. And then his father
died a decade later, and my grandfather, as the oldest
son, had to find the kind of job that could help support
his mother and younger siblings. He did, and the family
did all right. I would like to think that one act balanced
out the other—the act that wrecked the family home
and the one that helped rebuild their lives—but despair
plagued him so badly in later years that it seems the two
never carried equal weight.

For him, the tough times continued—he and his wife
could only have one child (the nights of miscarriages
were so hazy, my father had to learn about them decades
later from one of his mother's sisters), and then his wife
was diagnosed with cancer and given but weeks to live.
The disease went into remission and the weeks turned
into several years, but the toll of events, and the con-
straints on his imagination, sent him into a depression
that several times almost felled him.

Yet when all three were healthy—husband, wife, child—they built the cabin in northern Vermont, and with friends or alone, he fished the large, spring-fed pond, and penciled notes about his catch on the bare wooden walls.

A few casts with no response and I put on a darker fly, realizing, as I tighten the knot, that in truth I can but imagine the man, taking on the idea of him much like I pulled on the waders. I know he liked quiet water, and from there I fill in the blanks, seeing the promise under the stillness as a way to counter the despair that only electroshock treatments could finally jar out of him. Darkness inhabits our family's genes, and I have often felt it hover and spread, but pleasure in risk is coded there as well, which is what drew me to this stretch of river, with its steep banks and tumble of rocks, its fierce freshets and shoaly stretches. He, on the other hand, must have had to work hard to resist being impulsive, knowing too well how a split second can change a family's fortunes; he must have felt he had no choice but to make a career of being cautious.

Surely we share this, however; surely this moment is the same, whether on a river or a lake, when the right fly is on the line and a trout strikes it from below and swims hard away. It is then that every muscle preps itself for action, taut and aware of all that can go wrong—the hook isn't set right or the fish spits out the fly, or it tangles the line around rocks or is strong enough to break it with the right blast of speed. And here, of course, the bottom is slippery, footholds are tricky, and a false step could send me flailing downriver.

But at last the fish tires and is close enough to net, and I can see how my grandfather would handle it, admiring the heft, the flashes of silver and red. He, too, would inspect the lip for scars, the body for signs of previous catches. Then he would back out the hook, lower the fish into the water, and, in his cupped hands, coax it back and forth, back and forth, until its cells refilled with oxygen and it thrashed and was gone. I imagine it so because everything about this rod in my hand, the sun on my face, the net that looks like his, has me claiming it and him, along with the love of a wild thing that can feed one's very being.

I wonder what he would think of the catch-and-release rule on this section of river, where there will be no meal of trout at the end of the day, no delicate white flakes seasoned with lemon and butter. I like to think he would approve, not just for the life of the fish, but because of the shift it entails, creating a moment that can't be stolen, a record that can't be boarded over. It is, after all, the anticipation that keeps despair at bay, and the pull of line and slow cast and careful drop of fly. Little else matters when a breeze sweeps through the leaves, light scatters across the ripples, and a heron settles nearby, fishing its own stretch of water. Little exists then but the murmur of river and the hunger of lives just below the quiet surface.

Thoreau Alone Won't Do

THOREAU WAS IN MY pocket when I left high school in the early '70s, and in the years that followed, Thoreau has often been in my head, in the way we hang onto earlier teachers, even after we have outgrown them. "On Civil Disobedience" helped shape my thinking and ways of making decisions; so did Thoreau's use of walking and wondering to inform and frame his writing. When I'm on foot and alone, I welcome his presence, but when I roam to wilder places, where there is little trace of fields and farms, I need to hear footsteps other than Thoreau's beside me on the trail. I need guides who have known what it means to be a woman in far-flung places; I need the stories of those who prevailed in fraught or risky locations.

Of the three who show up most often, all, like Thoreau, were known for a refusal to conform. One was a seventeenth-century explorer who set sail—unescorted— for Suriname; another found a niche in photographing wild songbirds; and the third fashioned pants so she could be the first mountaineer to scale some of the world's highest peaks. The latter two, Cordelia Stanwood and Annie Smith Peck, never married, while Maria Sibylla Merian left her husband, with whom she had

had two daughters, and joined a sect that practiced celibacy, which finally convinced him to give her the divorce she had wanted. She was also a self-taught naturalist and artist, and, as a teenager observing silkworms, probably knew more about silkworm procreation than the leading male naturalists of her time.

I find a copy of the book she's best known for, *Metamorphosis Insectorum Surinamensium*, at the University of Massachusetts library, and handle it as carefully as the woman who retrieves it for me. Though the original was published in 1705—at the time, one of the largest books ever printed—this particular edition came out in France in 1775, with full-page illustrations that reveal Merian's artistry and interests. My translations are slow, but the gist of her discoveries is clear: Suriname ants thrill her as they "burst forth once a year in countless numbers from the cellars" and as they move from room to room in the house above, "sucking the blood out of any creature they meet, large or small . . . until even people have to flee," and as they move onto the next house, eating it clean as well. Tarantulas fascinate, along with the tales she hears about them. "When they fail to find ants, they take small birds from their nests and suck all the blood from their bodies." Sphinx moth caterpillars, when disturbed, release foam from their mouths, while bombardier beetles shoot excrement at those that might harm them.

She was, of course, mocked wherever she went—not only for refusing to accept the theory then circulating, that insects were formed via spontaneous generation, but also for trudging off into the forest with servants, a woman unescorted by a man of her class, in complete defiance of the customs of the other Europeans living in the Dutch colony, who were flush on the proceeds from the thriving sugar industry. Yet, despite the jeers and layers of heavy dress, the heat and sting of insects, she never seemed to waver, though in order to do what she did, as she once wrote a friend, "I almost had to pay with my life."

Linnaeus and Goethe recognized the value of her work, and her engravings so impressed Peter the Great that he assembled the largest collection of her art in the world, using it as the start of his Saint Petersburg museum. But the image I carry with me is of Merian in Suriname, clothed in pounds of heavy fabric, making careful notes after an arduous excursion ("I was obliged to walk behind some of my servants, who, hatchet in hand, opened a path for me with much pain") to return home bruised and dirty and quick to drop bugs into jars of preservative and tuck lizard eggs between layers of soft cloth.

Her ability to see what her contemporaries couldn't— as when she challenged the belief that insect life arose from putrid matter or that butterflies sprang fully formed from the mud—makes her an ideal presence when I am out on the trail. I, too, want to perceive what hasn't yet been seen, what conventional wisdom might otherwise keep me from noticing.

The second woman I often bring along, Cordelia Stanwood, accomplished her best work in June, at a time when blackflies are hatching by the millions in eastern Maine, their bites so relentless and fierce that they can make animals go mad, rushing wildly for water or mud thick enough to balm the painful welts. In his essay "Ktaadn," Thoreau described the blackflies of the

Maine woods as "more formidable than wolves to the white man." And yet there she was, spending days in the woods, keeping still despite fly swarms so that she wouldn't alarm the songbirds flitting ever closer to their nests. Most of her flesh was covered by Victorian attire, but the flies must still have found skin—nostrils, ears, forehead, scalp; it's what they do. With only a few weeks to find enough sustenance for their eggs, the flies need warm-blooded mammals, and humans are the easiest to access with their fine hair and thin skin.

Day after day, for hours at a time, Stanwood located and photographed birds and nests, often hiring local boys to help carry the heavy tripod or build blinds and a ladder when she needed something higher. She even resorted to using biting bugs to her advantage, as in the time she lured a young ovenbird to approach by offering it a dead mosquito. "After hesitating for a moment," she wrote in her field notebook, "it snapped it up. So then I put my hand flat on the ground and let the mosquitoes bite while the little bird walked over it . . . and snapped up the insects."

Eastern Maine isn't where she started her career, however; for the first twenty years she studied and taught art, and by the age of thirty-nine had worked in nine different school districts in Massachusetts, with no more than two years spent at each. In 1903 the hopscotching ended in what was described as a nervous breakdown, with several months of care in a sanitarium outside of Boston. It's not clear how much her collapse had to do with exhaustion and how much with the mentor she followed from district to district, but in the end, she returned to her family's homestead in Ellsworth, Maine, "confused but not confounded," writes her biographer, Chandler Richmond, "disillusioned yet not lost. Though she could not know it, there was still a half century of life awaiting her, by far the better part, beyond the spring."

The cure came with the waning of winter, when her horizon grew from a few small rooms to close to forty acres, all of which she soon learned in intimate detail. In the next four years, she managed to find and faithfully describe the active nests of one hundred different species of birds, a feat John Burroughs commented on with envy. Her field notebooks reveal the highlights of her days—a dime-sized warbler chipping free of its egg, a thumbnail-sized hummingbird just opening its eyes, a slew of fledglings drowned in heavy rains. As she would later write, "Nature will have all of our attention or nothing of you. If you think of yourself, or your affronts, you forget to look for the color, you lose the Cecropia's cocoon, you fail to see the bird or hear the song, and the flowers lose their fragrance."

She barely earned a living with her photos and writing, and refused all her neighbors' offers of help—milk, eggs, a dozen clams, a woodstove, a load of cordwood, a just-caught haddock. She sent the stove away and let the milk bottles freeze on the steps rather than accept any form of assistance from others. What soothed her came from her subjects, and when she writes about a thrush, singing at sunset, I feel she's describing my own experience.

When the thrush speaks to me, it seems as if the rags and tatters that enshroud my soul fall away and leave it naked. Then I must be simple and true or I cannot feel the message the small voice brings to me. When the thrush sings, I desire to live in a small, scrupulously neat camp, open to the sun and the wind and the voices of the birds. I would like to spend eternity thus, listening to the song of the thrush.

Reading her words, I, too, want to live simply again, remembering all those months on the Appalachian Trail and on other extended hikes, when I thrived on what I could carry on my back—a spoon, a knife, a sleeping bag, a bowl—with hundreds of miles of footpath ahead and few material possessions to weigh me down. They were easily the least complicated days of my life.

Stanwood's travel was considerably more laborious, burdened by the long black skirts and high-necked shirtwaists she wore until her death in 1958, but that didn't seem to limit her pleasure in pulling on hip boots and heading across swamps and over stone walls. She could easily be the person, rather than Thoreau, whom the biologist E. O. Wilson addresses in the letter that opens *The Future of Life* (2002): "When you stripped your outside obligations to the survivable minimum, you placed your trained and very active mind in an unendurable vacuum . . . In order to fill the vacuum, you discovered the human proclivity to embrace the natural world. Your childhood experience told you exactly where to go."

Like Maria Sibylla Merian, Stanwood models a way I want to pay attention, despite the real or perceived obstacles encountered along the way. As she writes in her field notebook:

Intimacy with nature is acquired slowly. It comes not with one year out of doors or with two. You look and listen, bewail your stupidity, feel that you have acquired little new information; yet, are determined never to despair or give up. All at once you know what you never dreamed you knew before . . . Yes, if you would study the secrets of nature, you must wear stout boots and a strong dress.

Kinglets; photo by Cordelia Stanwood

The third person to show up, Annie Smith Peck, understood all too well the role of stout boots and a strong dress, which I remember each time she appears, usually on rugged sections of trail—a steep drop-off on one side, narrow handholds on the other—or when I have to slow down to adjust a pack strap or catch my breath on a steep climb. It's then I sense her ahead of me, pushing hard for the top, her greatest goal the highest peaks that no one else had ever reached.

Yet it's not the record-breaking ascents that make her attractive, nor her refusal to be deterred by cost or logistics, traveling by steamer and mule, by horseback and rail, in one port even by barrel (the only way to reach a high-walled shore). It is instead the way she clothed herself—the gaiters and knickerbockers she wore in bitter cold and howling winds.

For every mountain Peck tackled, the arrangements were many and complicated—tents and guides, food and pack mules, clothing both for cold heights and for hot valley weather. People thought her mad, of course, blaming her rather than her hired guides when expeditions ended in failure. Her record ascent of Peru's Mount Huascarán—believed at the time to be the tallest mountain in the Americas at 22,205 feet—took six tries and ten years before she finally reached the top. And even that attempt, like many of her earlier climbs, was nearly ruined when a guide lost one of her precious mittens and then dropped both of his own on the descent, resulting in frostbite that led to later amputation of his fingers. His worst blunder, however, was when he hurried ahead as they neared the top of the mountain, so that it would be he rather than she who stepped first on the summit.

But from this remove, what matters more is not who was first, but that she was the first woman, in specially made pants that enabled each of her ascents: the Matterhorn in Switzerland in 1895 (14,691 feet); Orizaba and Popocatépetl in Mexico in 1897 (18,700 and 17,887 feet, respectively); and two of the six summits of Nevado Coropuna, Peru's highest peak (21,079 feet) in 1911, where she planted a "Votes for Women" pennant. She donned them for her two attempts on Mount Sorata in Bolivia (21,409 feet), as well, where she managed to reach 20,500 feet in 1904 before having to abandon the quest due to foul weather and a terrified guide.

Her approach to mountaineering was, like that to clothing, totally pragmatic. She never trained before a climb, though "I highly recommend such a course," she once remarked, "but for myself, except when I climbed to the Matterhorn, have had no opportunity." Upon reaching the base of a mountain, Peck simply commenced hiking, whether rested or not. She climbed despite deep snows and thin ice bridges, despite gear that was neither wind nor water repellent. She climbed on little food, on sufficient food, on chunks of chocolate and occasional coca leaves, reaching heights that no one had ever attained, in gale-force winds and brutal weather.

Her male companions were not as fortunate. Some of the more expensive ones—a university professor, a Swiss guide, a cocky muleteer—could not, at times, leave their tents due to altitude sickness. They quarreled with her over the best routes; they drank all the alcohol intended to fuel the stoves; they disappeared in the dark of night, leaving her to fend for herself. There were also the two men who watched her inch across an ice-coated ridge toward a summit they had lost the heart to reach, and then untied themselves from the life rope, without telling her what they were doing. Yet she kept climbing, a Vita Sackville-West without the sex change Woolf affords her in *Orlando,* striding along high mountain ridges and marveling at the fine views.

Like Cordelia Stanwood, Peck also taught for many years, before deciding, at age forty-five, that she wanted to climb the Matterhorn. She was only the third woman to reach the summit in the nineteenth century and the first to do it in the clothing that became known as her Matterhorn gear. According to Elizabeth Fagg Olds, who profiles Peck in *Women of the Four Winds,* "The audacity of [her] choice of costume can be judged by the fact that on the very day newspapers in this country [announced] her triumph, a woman was being prosecuted in Arkansas for appearing on the streets in bloomers."

By then, however, the act of climbing had exhilarated Peck, and she selected a mountain that had never been attempted. Though she wasn't able to reach the summit of Mount Sorata in Bolivia, on her descent she caught a glimpse of Mount Huascarán in northern Peru, with its massive rock faces and deeply fissured glaciers, and knew she would have to try for it. "A truly gigantic task," she would later write in *Harper's*, given the fact that "9000 feet of snow must be surmounted, of which the lower edge is higher than the loftiest elevation in the United States proper, and that the real climb begins only when one has surpassed the summit of Mount Blanc." Such an undertaking, she admitted, was "one of extraordinary hardship and difficulty."

Five times she tried and failed, and each time she learned more about both the mountain and the arduous task of raising funds to underwrite her climbs. She appealed to friends, to the famous, to magazines and geographic societies; she went on the public lecture circuit, offering such talks as "Afoot and Alone in Tyrol" and "Athens, The Acropolis, and Ten other Lectures on Greece."

Finally, in August 1908, she made her sixth attempt on Huascarán—her second attempt of the year—with two European guides and four local Indians, all of whom she had equipped with boots, long underwear, and climbing irons. She also had the Eskimo suit that Robert E. Peary used on his trek to the North Pole, and which he had urged the American Museum of Natural History to lend her, but it ended up at the bottom of a deep crevasse when a porter dropped it, along with all the supplies the man had been carrying.

Though the risks on each attempt were enormous—
violent weather, hundred-foot ice walls, whiteouts that
pinned them on perilous slopes—they reached the summit of Huascarán at last. It was the trip down that proved
the most dangerous of her life. As she described it in
Harper's, "My recollection of the descent is as of a hor-
rible nightmare." Blasted by high winds while fighting
for purchase on glassy slopes, she fell numerous times,
as did several of the others, each saved from thousand-
foot drops only by the rope that held them together and
the solid footing of those helping anchor it. The sturdy,
ever-optimistic Peck was almost undone. "Several times
I declared that we should never get down alive."

She made it, of course, and went on to receive a gold
medal from the president of Peru, a silver stirrup from
the Lima Geographical Society, and the honor, in 1928,
of having the north peak of Huascarán named after
her. In the subsequent years, she continued to seek out
new adventures, including flying over South America—
twenty thousand miles in over a dozen different kinds of
planes—as a way to celebrate both her eightieth birthday
and the relative ease of this new means of travel.

But it's the mountaineering Peck I like best, the one
who found a place on the globe that tested all her wit and
mettle. In her pants and tall boots, her stride and forti-
tude, she has become a companion on the tough patches,
which has often made all the difference.

After a Sweet
Singing Fall Down

1.

Blowing out eggs is a delicate affair, which I know from
handling those of chickens, during the summer we cured
a flock of eating each other's. We blew out the contents—
a pinhole in each end, a tight seal with the mouth—then
squirted in hot sauce, waxed over the holes, and returned
the rigged eggs to their nests to watch the hens fall for
the trick.

The stakes are, of course, much higher with the shells
of wild songbirds. The collector, in this case my great-
grandfather, first had to know which week a certain
migrant returned in the spring, and where it took up
residence, and how quickly it built a nest and laid eggs.
He had to time the careful harvest of specimens for his
collection before many cells had started dividing, and he
had to do it all during the busiest time in a farmer's year.

He must have gathered hundreds, for surely some
were too old and couldn't be blown; or they broke in
his coat pocket as he scaled a fence or crawled through
scrub; or he pressed his lips to the egg and his pinch was
too hard, his breath too strong, and the fragile shell gave
way beneath his working man's grip.

But dozens survived, from warblers and thrushes and sparrows and finches, and these he carefully labeled and nested in excelsior, the boxes packed as though readied for shipment to a museum. He didn't record the narratives—the swale where a rare bird's nest was found, the tree he had to climb, the angry parent he had to duck. Those stories died with him, and then the eggs were just eggs, and years later my grandmother, the logical inheritor, quietly and efficiently destroyed them.

She never said whether or not it was a hard thing to do; she may simply have become aware that it was illegal to hunt or own migratory birds or keep any part of them in personal collections. Or she may have found it a burden—having married by then and had two children of her own—in a world where nostalgia or sorrow had no role. Still, I wonder what passed through her mind as she obliterated the hollow eggs. Was it like the letting go I have had to do in the months since she died, of old notes and letters and slips of papers that she kept, listing birds she had seen on a certain summer day? Was it a last goodbye to the private conversations she and her father had shared—and that soon she and I would share—talks coded in bird names and habits and habitats?

Or had they simply become dusty, fifty-year-old eggs that ceased to suggest journeys or the potential for wild, vibrant lives?

2.

Spring birds sweep through the skies, hundreds of thousands in all colors and sizes. The nights are as busy and loud as the days while South and Central America empty of their transients. Sleep is difficult, and I want to spend all the lit hours outside, the house and surrounding land

seeming smaller under the sheer number of bodies passing overhead—warblers and thrushes and orioles and tan-
agers. Then I hear the chittering of freewheeling chimney
swifts, a call easy to distinguish above the other neighborhood voices, and I let them embody the flurry and pace
of the season.

The swifts' shape limits and makes possible everything they do, from their darting-fast flights to their de-
pendence on vertical walls. That last fact I learned as a
child while at my grandparents' cottage near Plum Island, Massachusetts, on a day too cold to be outside for
long. We had built a fire in the fireplace and gathered in
front of it with games, unprepared for the fall of baby
birds and their thin nest onto the edge of the grate, the
twigs shiny with the spit the parents had used to glue
them to the flue. We hadn't known the birds were there
or that they relied on chimneys and thus on us—an ig-
norance that for a while made us seem clumsy and brutal. But then, of course, we were kids and, until the fog
lifted, there was Monopoly to play, and crazy eights, and
soon enough we were back in the tidal pools or digging
enough sea worms so that Grampa could take us out to
the number two buoy, where flounder might bend our
poles into flailing half-circles.

The pirouetting birds I watch now make flight look
as easy as blinking, which, for them, it is. It's what they
do. Nearly tailless, with feet designed for clutching sheer
walls instead of walking, they spend their entire wak-
ing lives on the wing. They eat and drink and court and
mate, in flight; they break off twigs for their nests while
flying past bushes, and they keep track of each other
across great stretches of sky. When it comes time to die,
they even do that in the air, oblivious to life down below.

Rachel Carson, who wrote about them while working for the U.S. Fish & Wildlife Service, asserts in "Ace of Nature's Aviators" that the chimney swift "may be less aware of the earth and its creatures than any other bird in the world."

At night, they come to earth and settle into chimneys or hollow trees, leading a communally lived life except during the four to six weeks shared primarily with a mate. At sunset, anywhere from a few dozen to several thousand can pack, shoulder to shoulder, into a single flue—pulsing, restless bodies that breathe together until dawn. Then, one by one, they lift through the opening and scatter, their voices and flight patterns creating a wide net across sky.

Their aerial lives and ease with each other may account for their seeming absence of fear, which, for the earthbound, is a tough trait to fathom. Yet by all accounts I've read, when a swift is caught and handled, it tries to cuddle rather than escape, a fact Arthur Cleveland Bent clearly found odd. "They show little fear (consciousness) and appear tame to an extraordinary degree." In a story he relays about swifts taken from a trap, the birds snuggle into the kids' hands or hang onto their clothing, becoming breast-pins and pendants and reluctant to be pulled off. The terror seen in most caught birds wasn't present—the racing-wild heart, the flailing attempts to escape. The swifts simply waited until they could be airborne again.

But even the sensitive and brilliant Bent didn't know the answer to another mystery about swifts—about how they spent their winters and where it was they went. Perhaps their chittering couldn't be heard above the din of a rainforest, or the canopy was too thick to see a stubby

five-inch-long shape above it. But their annual absence
from the United States kept an old mystery alive, and
"even eminent naturalists of the past generation," as
Carson reminds us, "fell back on weird Medieval theo-
ries, such as the one that the birds buried themselves in
the mud of swamps and hibernated until spring."

3.

By the time I was six and old enough for dawn walks with
my grandmother, she had already discarded her father's
collection of eggs and spent years studying with a handful of serious birders. The eight of them were competitive enough to be excellent, but so cohesive as a group
that they made sure everyone saw everything—even me,
the lone kid, the few times I accompanied them on bird
walks, and I learned more from their remarks than I did
from poring over field guides.

Collectively, they were all such realists that each
would have scoffed at the idea of birds overwintering
in mud or otherwise hibernating in frigid states, just as
did the naturalists who preceded them—Izaak Walton,
Gilbert White, William Bartram, Robert MacLeod. Of
the latter group, however, none was comfortable denying that such a possibility could exist. Too many sane
and sober people had borne witness, they said; or, as
MacLeod once wrote, "If reputable persons have not
lied to me, then swallows do pass the winter like frogs."
Maybe, just maybe, as White intimated, there really was
a nearby *hybernaculum,* for no sooner would someone
insist that the idea of birds hibernating was as idiotic
as the one about their wintering on the moon than a
handful of chilled swifts would be found in a chimney
pipe, lifeless until warmed by the fire; or a tree would

be felled in February, packed with swifts that came alive in someone's warm hand; or swallows appeared near a brook in the spring, and no one could explain why they looked so slimy and disheveled.

A mental scrambling had to occur for those who looked on. It is, after all, cold-blooded things that freeze—like the spring peepers that wait, still as ice in the leaf litter, until the nights become warm enough to release them into action. Birds, for the most part, evolved to depart when cold arrives and food supplies dwindle, migrating thousands of miles to find warmth and good living. The ones that stay have to maintain active, heat-producing states, like the chickadees that pick around for seeds and insects all winter.

Or at least that was the long-held belief.

4.

When swifts mate, it's so brief that it's hard to believe anything happens. I have to watch for several hours to confirm that moment of contact, when the V of one bird fits onto the V of the other—a quick, cupped affair, a brief cloacal kiss, before each darts away as though nothing had happened. The speed is typical of all they do— single swifts having been clocked at 100 mph—which makes their daytime habits hard to study, their winter behavior even harder. "For five months [the swift] vanishes as utterly as though he were wintering on Mars," wrote a reporter for the *New York Times* in 1915. "Did they drop in the water or hibernate in the mud . . . their obliteration could not be more complete."

Their night-roosting habits, however, make them easy to capture, which is what researchers finally did, for ten years during the 1930s and early '40s, in what was, at the time, the largest bird study ever conducted. Balanced on rooftops in cities across the Eastern United States, dozens of volunteers captured and banded swifts as they departed their chimneys for the day. All told, close to 375,000 birds were tagged, though it took nine years from the project's start before the results finally came in—thirteen bands delivered to the American Embassy in Peru, all from birds shot in the Amazon Delta. According to Rachel Carson, death brought "ornithological fame" to those thirteen, for in their dying, they "filled in the missing paragraphs in the biography of their race." A sigh of relief must have passed through the scientific community, for this, Carson was convinced, would put to rest once and for all the myth of bird hibernation.

5.

I think it's fair to say that my grandmother had no apparent wish to practice or know feelings, having grown up in rural New England in a family where hard work and education were the primary ethos. The loss of two younger brothers, each dying shortly after birth; the stillness of the quarantines she twice had to endure; and the solitary days spent as a new wife, forced to give up her teaching career as soon as she married, must have confirmed the pointlessness in cultivating emotions. I saw her cry but once, when her husband of seventy years died, and my siblings and I, along with our mother before us, knew to be wary when describing the dramas of our lives, because a bird flying by could end a conversation, everything stopped until she could name it and make its connection.

How much better, then, to join with her in her interest rather than compete with birds for her attention. I grew to like the ways they pulled her outside and into new places, and I ceased to mind the fact that birds proved more fascinating than the feats or deeds of our family, because there they were: Geese that can reach altitudes of thirty thousand feet! Terns that can travel fifty thousand miles in a year! Shorebirds that can fly for nine days without food or drink or rest!

"The more astonishing, the more true," as one of Andrea Barrett's characters says in "Rare Birds," a short story I wished I had discovered in time to share with my grandmother, especially those last months of her life when I often read aloud to her. I like imagining my grandmother with a genetic link to the main characters, two women whose friendship blossoms through their shared love of natural history, and who bristle at the notion that some birds are able to spend their winters on lake bottoms.

Applying Barrett's twentieth-century logic to their eighteenth-century dilemma, the women set out to prove that birds cannot survive underwater. Their scheme is relatively simple: hire the gardener's son to capture swallows at night, then empty his sack into a barrel of water, which they then enclose with a net and boards. ("Everything happens so fast, a flurry of hands and cloth and netting and wings, loops of string and snagged skirt.") The next morning they slip back to the stables at dawn and find just what they had expected: twisted bodies sprawled at the bottom of the cask. The women's work is not yet done, however, for then they roll up their sleeves, scalpels in hand, and prove the bodies contain no means to maintain life without breathing.

Though triumphant in disproving the men of their
time, including the much-esteemed Linnaeus, who believed in subaqueous hibernation, they cannot prevail
over a more insidious belief—that the findings of two
women can't be taken seriously—and so they pack their
bags and depart, leaving no forwarding address, and
we're left to wonder why so little changed in the centu-
ries that followed.

6.

When my mother was first in college, in the heady post-
war years, she fell deeply in love. Exuberance was in the
air, as were triumph and possibility, and my mother and
her lover caught that joyous wave, headed for a sure
future of domestic bliss—except that one night, when
she and he were walking hand-in-hand down a snowy
road together, a car hit them, throwing her to her knees
and killing him on impact. Just like that, the dream was
shattered, and she was left alone to figure out what to
do next.

She left college for a while and stayed at home, seek-
ing solace in the passage of time and in what had once
been familiar. She found some of that in her father, who
one night laid his hands on her shoulders, as she sat at
the table, and let her know through his touch that such
sorrow made sense. Her mother, however, before leaving the room, simply remarked that it was late and they
should all go to bed.

In my understanding of the story, this was not my
grandmother's only departure at a crucial moment in my
mother's life, for when she first learned about her daughter's new lover, and their happiness and all they hoped

for, she waited until my mother had finished sharing the news and then pointed out a bird flying by the window.

7.

I have held wild birds and felt their fierce will to flee, and watched them try to find an exit from a house they had erred in entering, and heard them call in the predawn dark, so loud and alone that it seemed they would be owl meat soon, only to hear the same bird call again the next day. I know them as much by their vitality as by their coloring and size, which means I share the surprise of the man who put an injured nighthawk in the freezer (he thought it was almost dead and this would speed up its dying), and the next day he took it out and it moved in his hands.

It seemed implausible and yet I believed him; I had no reason not to, especially with his story ending well, with the bird flying away once he brought it outside. Had I been alive in earlier times, I might even have believed the stories then circulating, such as the account of two men digging in a salt marsh near Cambridge, Massachusetts, in February 1760, when they "dug up a swallow, wholly surrounded and covered with mud. The swallow was in a torpid state, but being held in their hands, it revived in about half an hour. The place where this swallow was dug up, was every day covered with the salt water, which at every high tide was four or five feet deep." A historian—Samuel Williams, a Harvard professor and a man of facts—had recorded the event, which had a definite impact on every naturalist who came after him.

I might have been more leery, however, of the descriptions of Olaus Magnus, author of *History of the Northern*

Peoples, a fabulous mix of Scandinavian lore and customs and history. So much of what he chronicled proved true, and he had a remarkable ability to create accurate maps, but who knows what he saw or heard in the early 1500s that shaped his understanding of the way certain birds prepare for winter. Swallows, in particular, he writes, were known to "clap mouth to mouth, wing to wing, and legge to legge, and so after a sweet singing fall down into certain great lakes or pooles among the Canes from whence next Spring they receive a new resurrection."

8.

The January nights were bitter and brilliant when my grandmother lay dying. The full moon lit up the snow and created a soft glow in her room, especially around the one window she kept open when she slept. The family maintained a vigil by her bed for the long days of her letting-go, and I took the night shift for its stillness and the chance to spend such silent time with her alone. The dining room clock chimed the quarter hours and occasionally she uttered something—"David," when her son told her he was leaving for the evening; "Catherine" when he told her I was staying; and, at one point, when snow blew around the house and the light outside was glittery and sharp, "It was a beautiful day. I spent it on Plum Island," and I could see her in the much loved place, wandering the fine sand beaches in search of terns and gulls and sandpipers; or taking a trail through the woods looking for warblers or an owl; or setting aside her binoculars on the slower summer days to fill a basket with the beach plums that she would later make into jelly.

Her breathing ebbed as the days drew on, and my youngest brother joined me at midnight, a welcome added presence in the long stillness. We took turns putting lotion on her skin, wetting a sponge to soothe her mouth, or reciting a favorite Psalm in the tick of slow minutes. Little else seemed to matter in the last hours of her life but that we be there, especially after that moment when, my hand on her shoulder, she turned and said, "Don't leave me." For the most part, I didn't, until that last day when I had to head out before dawn to teach the new semester's classes. But others arrived—my mother, my mother's brother, and the grandchildren who were able—and they were there when her body finally surrendered, which I sensed on my drive home, catching sight of a bit of rainbow through the flurries—the only color in the sky, illuminating a feather-shaped cloud.

She, of course, would have said little had I mentioned such a sighting, as in those times when I brought up dreams or talked hunches or bent down for a four-leaf clover, knowing a dose of luck could only help. She would have let the moment pass and then resumed an earlier conversation, about the health of turkey poults or the complications of global warming or the effect of a cold front on the next wave of migrating warblers.

9.

The poorwill, a night-flying, insect-eating bird, pirouettes nearly as fast as a chimney swift but has a much larger mouth, which functions like a scoop. On a cold winter day in the 1940s, in the Chuckwalla Mountains of California, the naturalist Edmund Jaeger found a torpid poorwill, a close relative of the whip-poor-will, tucked into a crack in the desert's rock walls. He found it or another bird in the same place, when he returned a few weeks later with several students, but though they handled it and shouted at it and opened and closed its wings, the bird couldn't be roused. Jaeger soon learned that the Hopi name for poorwill is "the sleeping one," and a Navajo boy, when asked about the birds, said that they could sometimes be found fast asleep in the nearby rocks.

For Jaeger it was proof at last that birds are able to hibernate. For others, it took decades and the advent of tiny transmitters, tucked into almost as tiny backpacks, to confirm what the Hopi already knew. In a study of poorwills, in the hills of southern British Columbia, a researcher caught and outfitted birds with the tiny packs, finding that at night their body temperatures dropped a staggering sixty-three degrees (from 104 degrees Fahrenheit to 41), a cascading that would kill a human being. A related study, on poorwills near Tucson, has found that they can remain in such a chilled state for weeks, a kind of Rip Van Winkle stasis, with no apparent delays when shifting from stalled state to full functioning.

In the years since, experiments have taken place around the world: birds chilled in labs and deprived of food (they settled into a sleep state); torpid birds targeted with loud noise or sudden bright lights (they might briefly open an eye); sleeping birds knocked over on their perches (they don't let go). The list of species believed to hibernate keeps growing, and ornithologists now believe that hummingbirds may enter torpor every night of their lives.

None of this can explain Olaus Magnus's operatic farewell—the in-sweep of wings like the closing of a cloak before the bird disappears into a pool among the canes— but it helps resolve at least some of the puzzle. When temperatures drop, some birds may appear dead, only to resume active life when there is warmth and food again.

Yet much of the puzzle still confounds: What to make of the stories of birds seen underwater, clutching grasses in their bills as the waters raced by, or of birds dug out of river mud in the coldest of days? Is there something we can't believe about the thing that animates them, our disbelief perhaps blinding us to all they are able to do?

10.

One doesn't really cry when a hundred-year-old person dies; it's more of a tender farewell that was long in the forming. Yet hardly a day goes by that I don't miss her—when I sit at the drop-front desk I inherited, near her pens and careful cursive; or hear the swifts overhead, queuing up for their trek to the Amazon; or follow a link to a website she would have enjoyed, as when I found the slowed-down version of a veery's song, one of our favorite birdcalls, inside it a complex melody that the human ear cannot hear without the aid of computers. She and I may not have said much about the matters of our hearts but in the language of birds we shared plenty.

I think of her now as I do the swifts, with their spit-and-twig nests and their preference for sky over land, and I know my ache when missing her is more akin to that of Arthur Cleveland Bent as he struggled to make sense of the swift's lack of interest in people. "How do we regard this bird that does not know we are on earth . . . a guest that does not know we are its host. We may almost think of it as a machine for catching insects, a mechanical toy, clicking out its sharp notes."

His tone of lament is as much for their indifference as for the ways they remain beyond our knowing.

Wild Geese and
Other Nostalgias

GEESE CALL TO EACH other in the damp morning air, calling on me to rush outside for the sight of heavy bodies appearing through the mist. I want to wave from the dooryard and support them on their way south, a fellow traveler who understands the labor involved in such long journeys. And almost immediately I know I'm not ready for them to be here. I haven't had that last swim yet or spent enough hours harvesting vegetables from the garden. The geese, of course, don't care. *Ha!* their voices say, *snow and dark are just around the corner.* And I see cold bulking up, about to lumber in, along with that stark look of bare trees and gray-brown of the hills.

Yet all around is an August day ripe with green and laden vines. Fruit sweetens by the hour in air chirred by crickets and grasshoppers. These geese, finally out of earshot and no longer insisting I follow their progress, are from a resident flock that drifts back and forth from the lake to fields of corn to a nearby section of river. I've been tricked once again by their calls. I'm late in remembering that they won't migrate any farther than a close place of open water, and that, in recent years, they have become as numerous as crows, and for crows my response is entirely different. I watch *them* with some caution, especially when they gather by the hundreds, rowdy and omnivorous and able to wreck crops in short order. While their raucousness has always been with us, the muscle of their numbers is new, as is the speed of their destruction; in the past anyone could shoot a crow, any time of the year, which kept their flocks nervous and thin, but those days are long over.

Like the crows, geese today are multiplying faster than cities and towns can handle, which puts us in the awkward position of discovering we have loved the birds too well. No one wants to lose the thrill at seeing a dark V against sky, or feel the response to their wild cries— *The geese are on the move, all is right in the world.* But there's little reason to hold onto such an image much longer.

Of the twelve or so species of goose here when the Europeans first arrived, one didn't migrate (the giant Canada goose, *Branta canadensis maxima*), but stayed around all year, such a good source of toothsome flesh that it was quickly hunted to dangerously low levels. The others came and went, spring and fall, were slaughtered by the thousands, and made excellent roasts for holiday meals. Such carnage wasn't slowed until the mid-1930s, when a law finally limited the number that could be killed and banned the use of live decoys when hunting them.

The large game farms that had raised such birds— those wing-clipped and tethered geese that convinced wild flocks it was safe to land—had to release them, hundreds upon hundreds of no-longer-profitable birds. Newly freed and trained by that point to stay in one place, the geese might have filled most of the nearby lakes all by themselves, but Fish & Wildlife Services throughout the country weren't that patient. They wanted game birds for hunters, who in turn pay their salaries, and they wanted them soon, so they netted and trucked them to previous goose-free waterways around their states, and the geese quickly set up residence and delighted neighbors with their presence.

Then the math of it began to tell. One mated pair, in a mere ten years, can produce a hundred hungry, active goslings. And if, at the end of those ten years, each of the hundred finds a mate (from new stock arriving from some other pond), the number can jump to a thousand by summer's end. And if the offspring of the earlier offspring are also factored in, the number multiplies even faster. Of course, not all goslings survive to adulthood. Snapping turtles eat them; so do raccoons and coyotes and mink, provided they can get close enough when the goslings are still small, which isn't easy with geese, with so many adult birds scanning for danger, and each willing to rush animals as large as deer and elk.

Another result of all that unchecked growth: great quantities of goose shit. Each goose produces about 155 pounds a year, a greasy green product that people slide through at the beach and park, and which in turn launches sudden algae blooms in goose-visited lakes and ponds. The higher numbers of geese also mean a greater likelihood of impacts with planes, and the loss of winter crops, and gray goslings wandering golf courses with impunity, protected by laws that prohibit tampering *in any way* with a goose that wants to live in the neighborhood.

For too long, we have loved them unwisely.

Morning crests the hill in shades of gray and blue, while down by the river, mist steams on a day too warm for December. A few stems of aster are still in soft bloom below naked trees and bunches of withered grapes. Other than a few mallards, the hour is quiet, with distinct pockets of cold and warm air. And then I hear them approaching—a gang of boisterous geese somewhere in the mist—but this time I'm braced and know them as bowdlerized, an idea gutted of all that's mournful and seductive.

They don't fully materialize and I wander home, ready to roast some of the chestnuts I had gathered back in October from a neighbor's tree, a Chinese American hybrid that sprawls over our yard. A hard wind brought down most of them in one week and within minutes I had a basketful. Their taste is not as robust as the native chestnut, but it's still a good and sweet flavor that will complement supper.

When I lift the basket, however, I find chunky white grubs underneath. Lots of them. I shake the basket and more fall out and then I see the holes drilled into each nut: the mark of the chestnut weevils that got to them first. Months ago, the adults buried their eggs when the fruit was still forming, and now the young are eating their fill of nut meat before boring their way out and humping across the floor, a trail of pale dust behind them.

I give up on finding clean ones, toss the lot into the compost, and go instead on a hunt for more geese stories.

It seems there is no way to write about them other than with a tug to the heart. Even the unsentimental Edward Forbush, writing about birds of the Northeast, couldn't resist poetic references to geese: "Coming after the long,

cold winter, not even the first call of the Bluebird so stirs
the blood of the listener." Geese conjure the rhythm
of seasons and an idyllic rural past, which we reenact
each time we reach for an oil lamp, a hand-cranked corn
husker, a penny postage stamp. Nostalgic for a simpler
time, we let geese carry our imaginations from winter to
summer grounds, from hard times to better, though doing so now is akin to singing about sleigh rides in places
that never see snow, or shopping for balsam wreaths and
Christmas trees in South Florida. Though current estimates vary widely, experts now agree that resident geese
far outnumber those that migrate.

I flip more pages, wondering whether other birds elic-
ited the same emotional responses from Forbush or his
correspondents, stopping people in their labors so they
could lean back and scan sky. The snow goose was one, a
bird that V's over like the Canada goose but is a higher
and quieter flier, with a more nasal than musical honk.
It was here in the thousands when Europeans were first
arriving, yet already rare when Forbush began compil-
ing his notes in the 1920s (the "banks of birds melted
quickly . . . before the incessant flashings of the white
man's gun"). Though its numbers have since recovered,
the temporary absence had a brutal effect on the Indians
along the Hudson Bay, who depended on them for food.
According to Forbush, without the predictable, seasonal
return of snow geese, many Native Americans faced subsequent starvation.

Another once-regular migrant, the whistling swan,
is twice the size of a Canada goose and has a lush, bu-
gling call. "To an ornithologist," writes Forbush, "there
is no more thrilling sight than that of the flock far up in
the azure heights, their long necks stretched toward the

pole, their glistening white plumage catching the rosy rays of the sun. . . . [Yet] in New England we rarely see or hear them now." Their numbers soon rebounded, though not to their earlier numbers, while a close relative, the trumpeter swan, never recovered from the heavy hunting pressure and is now known to most of us through E. B. White's children's book *The Trumpet of the Swan.*

In recent years, another species—the mute swan—has been imported from Europe as part of the ongoing campaign to keep Canada goose numbers in check. It joins a long list of other goose-deterrents, including recordings of loud explosions played at unexpected times, foul-tasting chemicals sprayed on the grass where geese feed, and border collies trained to chase them off runways. (The plan proposed in some cities, such as happened in Detroit—kill the offending geese and give the meat to food banks—infuriates animal-rights activists; in Illinois, they charged the state with delivering "environmental toxins" to unsuspecting citizens. Geese that fed locally, they claimed, were loaded with pollutants, and feeding them to people was like supplying "chemical-biological weapons under the guise of welfare.")

Unfortunately, the imported European swans, which have proven effective at attacking geese, are proving equally effective at assaulting humans. Anyone who has seen a mute swan rush a person knows that Leda didn't have a chance against Zeus, when he raped her in his swan's shape and spawned mortals.

Hundreds of geese have gathered on the ice, angled and elegant against the setting sun. The low rays of February exaggerate their size, each white chin abnormally large in the steam the birds generate. I roll down the car window, from a nearby pull-off, and a dozen geese tense and lengthen, their erect necks like arms in elbow-length black gloves, an effect both sturdy and sensuous. And then something startles them, something beyond the point of land, a dog perhaps, or a kid throwing rocks, and the geese jerk to their feet and honk and flap to the far side of the cove. I head back to the road but can't shake the image of geese over black water, or the power of their hold on me. I'm still not sure how to love them less, or how to love them differently.

The dilemma reminds me of the conflict Mary Oliver sees in the work of Robert Frost, where there's always some lament, she says, some itch or dissatisfaction. And yet there is also something lyrical and comforting as well, so that two messages come at us at the same time— "*everything is all right,* say the meter and the rhyme; *everything is not all right,* say the words." (Geese are gorgeous, say their wingbeats; geese are dangerous, say their size.) While themes of death and despair appear again and again in Frost's work—of the hired man, the young boy injured by a saw, the lonely hill wife who disappears into the woods—"whatever disappointments and woe Frost felt," Oliver writes, "he rocked his way through them and made the perfect cages of his poems to hold them." The resulting lines are dark and light, haunting and musical, brutal and soothing all at the same time.

I feel the same rocking moment with these geese—handsome and rowdy as they skein across crimson sky, their voices both lonesome and brash. Just as on some days I can't bear to read more Frost, there are also those times when I am back inside his vision, watching a white spider or hearing an ovenbird, feeling the same bittersweet sensations as when losing more chestnuts or living through a fall that's not a fall without high flying geese.

I seesaw back and forth with these solid-bodied birds, in a complicated relationship that for now we cannot escape. They're like that branch of the extended family whose lives suddenly turned ugly, yet we can't forget that we are kin and that we are in this together, and for now I am in no hurry to surrender the better memories.

When a Fox Skull
No Longer Points Home

IT IS THE QUIET time of year—no leaves, no insects, no birds or nattering of squirrels. In these woods, the snow cover is deep, and it contains and subdues most sounds, an absence that has its own weight and against which my snowshoes rattle. The few noises arrive with the first fall of flakes—a just-audible nick against branches and needles. Then comes the shift of new snow, sliding off limbs, off my coat, off the stiff beech leaves that won't drop until spring.

I snowshoe on and locate an animal's slide—not long like an otter's and nowhere near water—and figure the track to be that of a fisher, an animal that's not supposed to be here in the Northeast, at least according to any guidebook published before the last decade. Fishers, dark and powerful members of the weasel family, are supposed to inhabit the far northern boreal forests, not these hills rising between the Connecticut River and the taller Berkshires to the west. Yet one has been here, and it has been busy, zigzagging back and forth in search of prey, then wandering through deeper snow, leaving a long belly scrape. I follow the trail another fifty feet until it disappears under a hemlock branch so laden with snow that it rests on the ground like a hand.

I lift the branch and feel as though I'm entering the privacy of a bedroom. I can see where the animal curled in sleep, the curves of its body imprinted on snow that its heat melted. Its smell fills the small chamber, a musky scent so rank and strong that I know it would take but seconds for it to coat me were I to drop the screen of needles and roll onto the bed. Instead, I snowshoe home, startled at how ready I was to move into the animal's realm.

For a long time, I thought I could live anywhere, that home was wherever I found myself—a town, a city, an island, a tent, an apartment, a fixer-up place.

Then Holly and I set down roots on these several acres with the old house and barn, and my definition of *home* came to include the garden and flowers and best rooms for views, and the pleasure in knowing where the wild grapes hang, the red fox dens, and the lady's slippers reveal their erotic pink selves. Home became a happiness so wide I couldn't see anything outside my field of view. The sweetness of kale picked after the frost! The number of stars on the coldest nights of the year! The first fists of rhubarb, signaling spring!

It took at least a year to realize that the person I most wanted to share this with could no longer afford to stay; the cost to her heart had become too great, and I have no idea how to prepare for the possibility of leaving here.

Each time we fly to South Florida, for the first day or so
I see only bougainvillea in bloom, orchid trees laden with
blossoms that look ready for flight, and gardenia languid
with scent in bushes taller than I stand. It takes far longer
to see Miami's grid of streets, the high-rises downtown,
the stucco and tile inland, and the ever-changing styles.

When the noise and speed become too much, I scan
sky. I count vultures, sometimes three dozen or more
riding the thermals, an occasional frigatebird soaring
among them. Around us, cars and horns and alarms jam
the air. On the sidewalk, people give me a quick once-
over—I am tall and blonde, maybe a movie star, maybe
someone famous in this world of revolving chic—then the
look shifts. I'm not dressed quite right, I haven't taken
the proper care, and I become just another body in the
fast-moving crowd.

Everywhere people are talking, though most of it to
those not in view. Cell phones and thin microphones
send their stories and hot deals around the world, with
no time to lose. Everyone has a scheme in this city of
speculators, and they travel at the future's near edge,
where the present is already passé, and the scenes speeding by offer little relevance.

On the shaded streets, banyan trees lace earth to sky.
An opossum rocks across a backyard, its rolling gait welcome as a friend's laugh. In the cool of evening, shadows
create narrow alleys out of otherwise large walkways,
and the roadsides become less visible. I feel the shuttle
and chirr of insect life; I sense how the land that isn't
paved teems.

Near my stepdaughter Chandra's house, skinks leap
leaf to leaf, a walking stick separates its thin body from
twig, and the city becomes more bearable and green.

On a ridge in the town of Florida, Massachusetts, one of the coldest areas of the state, an old forest ages quietly, its granite ledges softened by a thin layer of lichens and ferns. Under one such rock ledge, porcupines have lodged for years. Their scat litters the floor, messiness typical of an animal that can sleep near its own shit or leave it in such heaps in the doorway that much spills back into the den.

In a corner of this particular cave, there is also a pile of quills, an intricate tangle, like a child's stack of pick-up-sticks. It's an odd arrangement amid the den's disarray, as though the animals had groomed themselves and swept up afterwards, setting aside anything that might be dangerous to the softer-skinned young. But porcupines don't indulge in that kind of tidiness; something else created this spiny mound.

Twenty feet away, I find one dying, its feet curled against its sides, lines of blood on its face, each blink of its eyes slow and labored. It may have fallen off a high branch, a not-uncommon fate for the clumsy animals, or it may have been forced off by the jabs of a fisher, the animal best designed to kill this well-armed prey.

Its method is slow but efficient. The fisher slashes at the porcupine's face and then beats a retreat. When the porcupine spins, trying to hit the fisher with its tail, the fisher leaps out of reach and slashes the porc's face again. And so they go in a kind of *danse macabre,* slash and spin about, slash and spin about, until the loss of blood take its toll and the porcupine no longer keeps up.

My arrival may have ended the dance. Had I not appeared, the fisher would have flipped the porcupine over and then skinned it, a slick everting of fur and quills, exposing an easy meal of soft body parts. And had that whole scene been played out in the den and the hide left there to rot, surely it would have left a pile of quills, just like the one in the far corner.

That's how I imagined it anyway, though the ranger stationed at the state forest headquarters can't confirm it; nor can the environmental police officer, with whom I talk a few days later. Even the famous tracker who lives nearby can't say with confidence that a pile of quills means a fisher kill. "Too little is known about them," he says, "other than that they're fierce and efficient and showing up all over the Northeast," and I think again of the comment made by a friend, who has caught fishers in traps meant for coyotes. "Their return," he says, "is like having another piece of our wilderness back."

It's a wildness I want as part of my idea of home, but when I try to define that for Holly, it's clear that, to her, wildness means violence, of which she's had enough.

On past visits to Miami, most of what I saw was artificial excess on an isolated stretch of waterfront, with little connecting the city to the rest of the United States. All seemed man-made, former swampland tamed by concrete and steel, by artificial turf and reprocessed coral reefs, a place where people spent most of their daylight hours inside, in air kept dry and well chilled. I had to work to find the places where wild inhabits the city, the only way not to feel rent between the way I want to love and my love of the land. The only way to keep grief from filling the rift.

For Holly, the city now seems comfortably tame, compared to the chaos that erupted when she was first there with two small children. The changes began when they were sleeping, or when she was arranging daycare for them, or while she was carrying home bags of groceries. Suddenly a car exploded at the turn of an ignition key; a mailbox detonated when kids were crossing the street; a helicopter dropped low and hovered overhead, people scattering under the bright lights as sirens wailed up her street.

It was the late 1970s and early 1980s, when drug dealers were defending turf, Anita Bryant was assailing gays, and cops along the Miami River were discovering how valuable were smuggled goods and how dispensable the smugglers. Extremism was in vogue and was the only acceptable reaction when Castro toyed once again with the United States, as in his allowing a mass exodus of Marielitos—purportedly criminals and the insane, the frightened and poor, an untidy wave of people in boats large and small.

Holly still looks stunned when reciting the short list of killings that occurred in those years—a man shot in her backyard; a friend's child murdered; a friend's husband murdered; a friend's fiancé murdered; a car bomb that blew the legs off a man for being a traitor to the anti-Castro forces. The gulf between the classes had grown so wide that rage was one of the few ways to cross it. Meanwhile, empty rafts drifted onto the beaches, Haitians who struggled ashore were sent home, and paperless Central Americans became the new slaves of the wealthy. For Holly, the imperious Orlando Bosch, selling fruit on the sidewalk in his court-ordered bracelet, was one of the last straws. The self-proclaimed terrorist had bombed a plane and a cruise ship, many people had died, and yet passers-by honked and cheered him from their cars, while the law dragged its heels because of its own complicity in abetting his crimes.

She wanted a safer place, where her nightmares could run their course and all the risk she would ever need would come from her own imagination. A few years after we met, we moved to a town with fewer than two thousand people, a hundred miles due west of Boston. Here, two brooks pass near us, quiet woods stretch to the east, and within a short while we knew most of our neighbors. It seemed a good place to recover from the trauma of mingling cultures.

Yet she still hovers over a map of Miami; I can feel it. When her son calls, she asks where he is so she can imagine the intersection, the sights from his car window, the blossoms of frangipani and royal poinciana coloring the ground, the air sweetly scented with mimosa. "What are you having for dinner?" she'll ask, so she can know where he and his new wife have shopped, what smells waft through their kitchen, what blend they're creating of Cuban and Anglo ingredients. The two move between Spanish and English as they speak—*pastelitos, croquetas,* fried bananas, ripe mangoes, Little Havana, the Grove, Calle Ocho—and I smell the hot, cement-block buildings and see the big skyline and long crawl of mangrove roots, the heaps of relentless green hacked back with machetes, and the wild things beating a fast retreat from long blades.

I enter the woods that I may soon leave, walking as though my body were unzipped and raw. It is not easy to love a person and a place in equal measure; it's tough to admit that my desire to be near her will mean severing my roots from this earth. I work to take heart from the fisher's return—change happens and that's a good thing—though in this waning fall air, hope is an elusive thing. Respite comes in the demand of my senses. I need to pay attention; I want to sense brook and deer and pine for as long as I can. And then I see a fox skull atop a scattering of oak leaves. It's clean of fur and facing south and looks tenderly, deliberately placed, and I don't know how I missed it earlier in the season. I had only to look a few feet to the left and I didn't.

I squat to see under the reach of low plants and find pelvis and ribs, lumbar strewn like beads, and a section of lower jaw, stained from oak tannin. Under a thin layer of dirt lies a triangle of teeth, startlingly white and scarcely worn, as though the animal were barely a year old, and I can hardly explain the odd pang I feel. I missed the moment when the fox breathed its last and that hurts far more than seems reasonable.

I scrape away earth but can't tell what caused its death. No bones seem cracked or shattered from impact; no bullets appear in the leaf litter. Instead, the curve of spine suggests a death in sleep, an animal tucked for the last time into the warmth of itself.

It seems it was just a few months ago that it barked outside the house, sometime in the night, and I didn't step outdoors to see what it wanted. And now I can't tell whether it was poisoned or weakened by disease, or whether a life spent as a fox was simply too exhausting and hard.

The den is barely one hundred feet away, under a canopy of white pines and black cherry trees. In this late autumn day, needles rain down in the breeze, a sound as thin as sleet but softer on my skin. I start to leave and then turn back, kneeling to fit my hands under the skull. I don't know where I'll store it or why I want to hold it. I know only that the animal died in the months when the den was active, when I watched a healthy fox carry in a ruffed grouse one day, a gray squirrel the next, and I forgot to watch what else was happening a short distance away.

I cup the skull in my hand as though it could help me know how to leave when the time comes. But on the long walk home all I can see are bones—in splintered mushrooms, in pale fern fronds, in the thin beech limbs that stretch across the trail.

The Quiet House Is a Sudden Thing

THE COFFEE FINISHES BREWING, the sky lightens to gray, and then the power zips out, fast as a caught breath. The night's hard storm has passed and there is but the occasional drip of rain on the roof, as we wait inside the shut-down house, sure the electricity will flick back on soon, the way it always does.

It doesn't. The moment lengthens, the quiet house a sudden thing, unlike the long dying of Holly's mother, the withdrawal of Holly's daughter, the growing of the tumor on the side of my knee. We saw each on the horizon for months, and yet they had beginnings, they had endings, we could chart our journeys through them, and though Holly still weeps at missing her mom, her daughter has yet to return a call, and thick staples run like a zipper down my leg, we have journeyed, like good travelers, along the road that takes us through them.

The silence builds like pleasure, a joke that takes a while to get. And then how joyous the sputter of candle wax; how sweet that the phone doesn't work or the link to the Internet. The refrigerator isn't humming, the furnace isn't blowing, the fluorescent lights above the sink emit no buzz. In the stillness, the greens out back seem brighter, the trees more vital, all of them shimmering in the early hint of sun.

We barely talk, the knock of spoons against cereal bowls as subdued as our voices. Without speaking, we say, *Let's stay home. Let's call in sick.* The quiet comforts, a physical thing we pull over ourselves, like fog, like that place just before we know all we wished we didn't.

Resilience

1. SUMMER STORM

The river has turned into a boiling brown force, a creature hulking above the banks, the rocks, the old bleached logs stacked for years along the shore. In the night, it roared through a nearby campground, giving people barely enough time to wake and flee their tents before it absorbed what was left—cameras, sleeping bags, stoves, wallets, clothing, food. It churned across roads, carried away culverts, and roughed up the footings of the bridges and trestles.

The gates at all the dams have been opened, and the boards meant to break away from the dam tops are gone. The upper reservoirs hold much of the excess, which keeps the towns themselves from being flooded, but below them nothing can slow all that water cascading through the valleys.

At Gardner Falls, just below our house, the river runs at nineteen thousand cubic feet per second, or about twenty-seven times its normal speed. It wrenches free the orange barrels, which warn boaters of the upcoming dam, and flings them downriver like corks.

Three towns declare a state of emergency. Sudden
gullies bisect roads, cutting off access to several homes,
with no one able to drive in or out until the holes are
patched. Road crews redirect traffic with cones and bar-
ricades, creating detours over narrowed ground still able
to support the weight of cars. Meanwhile, on the river
itself, rescuers scurry to pick kids out of trees, collect
people and their inner tubes off islands, and ferry back
the family that set out in canoes before the waters turned
dark, not realizing how fast the river was rising.

Despite the close calls, no one dies and no one is seriously hurt, due to a series of fast actions—the man who
lay on his car horn to wake sleeping campers; the man
who raced from tent to tent, slitting doorways open with
a knife; the passerby who spotted two girls trapped on
an island and placed the 911 call; the rafting guides who
plucked a naked man from a tree, where he had clung
since the wild current tore off his shorts.

There had been no coordinated alarm announcing
the rising waters, no town crier carrying the warning
downstream, nobody keeping others from launching a
boat, an inner tube, a raft. Just neighbors and rescue
workers and whitewater guides trained and living in this
area, loving and knowing and always wary of the river,
and then a heavy rain, way too much rain, and all those
people reacting as the river churned brown, scouring the
banks, the rocks, the small islands.

2. HEADWATERS

Everywhere we travel in this valley, on each ridge and
slope, there's evidence of the river's drain. It's in the air
we breathe, in the shapes of the towns, and in the sounds
that enter our houses at night. A river's tug is also in

the stories I have loved, of John Wesley Powell, paddling one-armed on the Colorado, of William Bartram on the St. Johns, Mark Twain on the Mississippi, and Kathleen Dean Moore on so many rivers of the Northwest. And, of course, Thoreau on the Concord and Merrimack in Massachusetts, on the Allagash and East Branch in Maine, and alongside a small pond for two years, forever linking a body of water with a way of inhabiting a life.

I imagine rivers shaping our very beings, until we're like salmon that have adapted to their natal waterways, wiry and strong where it's shallow and rocky, and bigger and slower in more languid streams. Though a person may have to remain in place for decades before it happens, I can already hear the river in the vernacular of friends, particularly those loath to attend events that take place outside their watershed.

In a hunt for more clues about the effects of the Deerfield, I wander through southern Vermont, searching for its origin. The going isn't easy; there is no bankside trail, no steady opening in the underbrush. There are the few access roads that crisscross this part of the Green Mountain National Forest, and occasionally there are moose paths, with signs of heavy browse and antler-scarred trees. But mostly I push through thick brush and unmarked areas, keeping close to the increasingly narrow waterway. In shaded areas the rocks are green with algae and moss, while the dark pools of water swirl with red and yellow leaves.

Soon the stream is so narrow, water striders cross it in several easy sweeps. A short distance beyond, I reach a level area of land, a small pond made by beavers in its middle. Balancing across a tangle of branches, I walk the perimeter, and find but a dozen dead trees, a silent

pair of wood ducks, and a thick muddy trough that a
moose has dug, and into which it has peed—or so the
smell says—as part of its claim to this place.

The lack of feeder stream means that somewhere inside this body of water a spring percolates out of the
ground—the northernmost source of what will become
the Deerfield, a river that drops roughly twenty-two hundred feet in elevation on its journey from here to the
Connecticut. It feels like reaching the story's first chap-
ter at last, which up to now I had been reading out of
sequence. It's like that moment years ago, when I stood
on the New Hampshire–Canada border and fit all of
what would become the Connecticut into the cup of my
hand, and then turned around, settled into a canoe, and
paddled its length to Long Island Sound.

I'm not sure how far I'll travel from here but decide to
trust my instincts, bushwhacking through the woods in
the direction of my car. I don't have a compass, and the
sky has become too overcast for shadows. Still, I want to
trust my sense of direction, as though I could follow my
notion of *east*. An access road is relatively close, and if I
veer too far to the north or west, I'll eventually meet the
well-marked Appalachian Trail, though that could take
more time than I have food or water to do easily. But
striking out like this seems worth the risk, there's plenty
of sign of deer and ruffed grouse, and the hobblebush
berries have begun turning red.

It doesn't take too long before I can't tell where I'm
going; I can't see far enough in any direction to know
if I'm pursuing a straight line, and there's no height of
land to afford perspective in these thick woods. There's
just a light area in the distance that may or may not indi-
cate the cut of the road.

And then I see the stream ahead, a place I passed earlier in the day. The rocks look familiar, as does the spill
of current over a long flat stone. I have walked in a big
half circle, as though my body were pulled by a gravita-
tional force rather than a magnetic one, and it moved
downhill like water, as in that predawn hour when Holly
and I hauled our sleeping bags to the meadow to watch
the best meteor display in recent history, hundreds of
light streaks parting black sky. Two of us, cocooned in
fat bags, awed and silent and sliding slowly toward the
brook at the bottom of the field. It was the slipperiness
of our sleeping bags. It was gravity's pull. And it was the
draw of water, which our bodies couldn't resist.

3. ROTENONE

Following the questions backward—how do we come to
know a river, how does a river shape us—means going
beyond all that draws the tourists and artists and swim-
mers to the Deerfield today, and spending time with
the river when little about it was poetic. Though it had
long been seen as muscle to be harnessed, with mills and
shops and waterwheels along its shores, there was also
a time when it was simply the great flush, when sewage
pipes emptied directly into it, spilling all the waste from
houses and factories, restaurants and laundries—shit and
chemicals and soiled papers and fabrics, oils and deter-
gents and contents marked "poison." The mess was once
so great and the pipes so many that WPA laborers, who
were sent in the 1930s to count them, described scenes
that became increasingly odious: "[I]t may be said that
sewage is discharged promiscuously . . . in such manner
in some locations that a misstep may take the pleasure
away from an otherwise enjoyable fishing trip."

There was even a time when the life of the river was seen as something humans could control, which I discover as I sort through issues of *Massachusetts Wildlife* from the midcentury. At the time, the waters of the Deerfield, slowed and warmed by successive dams, were no longer supporting trout, which like the chilliest of streams. As a result, so-called trash fish had moved in and taken over most of the fishing holes, and the trout just couldn't compete. Despite the replacements the state emptied into the river each spring—one hundred thousand or more, all healthy and hatchery-raised—less than 50 percent were caught by the anglers whose license fees paid the salaries of the Fish and Game employees. The others were outmaneuvered by the sunfish and shiners and suckers and carp that moved about more easily when the summer sun heated the waters. After several months of public debate, the officials decided to take action.

They opted for the total-eradication, start-all-over method, with rotenone as their poison of choice. An organic substance made from various tropical plants (jewel vine, derris, hoary pea), rotenone is used by lots of farmers and gardeners. When sprayed on fruits and vegetables, it kills harmful insects without injuring the plant. When poured into water, it kills every bug and fish that swims there. Supposedly, neither people nor pets are affected (though a bit of time in a library yields a study of laboratory rats that showed all the symptoms of Parkinson's disease after rotenone was introduced into their bloodstreams. "The best model we have ever had," says one of the participating researchers, "for this disease being associated with an environmental agent").

Fifty years ago, no one suspected impacts on human or animals, and with the best of intentions, the state wildlife agency poured rotenone into the Deerfield, just below Sherman Reservoir, and into several of the feeder rivers—Clesson Brook; the Cold, Chickley, and South Rivers; along with both branches of the North River and a few smaller streams. An estimated seventy-five thousand pounds of fish—thirty-five different species—were killed, including fourteen hundred pounds of trout. Cleanup crews took to the shores—fisheries personnel, citizen volunteers, and inmates from the nearby work camp—netting and shoveling great quantities of dead bodies, which were then dumped in huge pits and buried by bulldozers.

The result was a sterilized environment, which stayed empty a few hours, a completely stopped moment in the life of a river. Then a hundred thousand hatchery trout were released into the flushed-clean water, with a similar amount added the next spring. Insects had to come in on their own, whirligigs and damselflies, water striders and caddis flies, along with all the algae and bacteria and crayfish and snails that had to float down from Vermont, drift in on other streams, or catch a ride, if they were able, on a duck or a turtle.

For a while, the trout fishing was splendid, thousands of fish caught by countless happy humans. But no natural force could hold back the arrival of competitors; no hand could maintain such artificial conditions; the dams had changed it to a warmer body of water. Less than fifty years later, most of the undesirables are back—sunfish and shiners and suckers and carp—the river populations having reverted to their own states of balance, their own ways of responding to food supplies and predator-prey relations and fluctuations in temperatures.

Rotenone is still used by fishery managers across the country when they want to clean bodies of waters of introduced species or unchecked disease. Sometimes there's no other choice, they say, but to kill everything off and start over. But surely this couldn't happen again to a *river*, rotenone spilled into water that flows past drinking supplies and market gardens, into water we wade in and fish from and bask alongside.

Surely it couldn't happen now, with the way people watch like vigilantes. They come from all over to see the Bridge of Flowers and Glacial Potholes, the picnic areas and churning falls, and want the river as healthy backdrop in their photographs and videos. Those living within sight of the river have spun around their home's orientations; instead of facing away from what used to be more septic than clean, now they want to see the river every time they look out a window, and anything out of the ordinary has them networking with others. An odd sheen, an ill duck, a dozen fish floating belly-up, and people are on the phone to local officials and environmentalists, knowing too much about DDT, PCBs, and *Silent Spring* ever to be so complacent again.

4. THE SLIDE

A wet animal has padded through town, loping around the falls, the parking lots and businesses, the pull-off where parents rock children in strollers, leaving its damp-feet evidence, a line of drips off its tail, which I follow shortly afterward, until I come upon the evidence that can only mean *otter*.

A few days earlier, I had watched one on the river's far side, feeling its way around roots and snags, reaching under rocks, snagging a crayfish, maybe a frog. Sinewy and lithe, larger than a mink and narrower than a beaver, it was all about focus and the abundance of crannies.

But following its tracks to the top of this slide—a slick path that leads straight from the bank top to the water— is what brings all the pieces together. We have a resident otter, and it's dividing its time between eating and sleeping and play.

I stand on the bank and imagine it journeying out of sight of the town center and then sensing a certain shape to this steep bank. It scrambled up from the river, inspected the pitch, and then, at the top of the slope, its sleek body poised, it flopped onto its belly, stroked twice with its feet, and became both sled and operator, both luge and a kid in unimpeded flight. It hit the water with a splash and within seconds reappeared and looked around, as though to see who might have noticed and thought the entry well done. Then it was back up the bank to do it again, the dampness of its body like wax on a toboggan.

The freshness of the tracks make the story easy to read, the pleasure so fine that were it hot and I much younger, I, too, might want to test this slope for its speed. Though it is, of course, uneven and muddy, with poison ivy and downed branches on either side. But the slide of an otter suggests *joy* and *play*, words we rarely apply to adults of any species, whose lives have grown serious with the needs of survival. A slide is a reminder of the way otters *frolic*, despite trappers and hard times; of the way they *cavort* and dive for pebbles and take apart clams while floating on their backs; of the way they seem *capricious* and *carefree*.

And *culprits*, as many around here believe, taking more than their share of fish, including the tiny salmon launched by kids from the local elementary school, who watched eggs turn to fry in small tanks in their classrooms. Otters have twenty-four-hour-a-day access to rivers, and sudden, rushing tides don't deter them. They wade when it's shallow and wait when it's too fast. They swim under ice and burrow into banks and get first dibs on the brook trout that the state delivers each year, tossed by bucketfuls into the river from the hatchery truck tanks. Sometimes they even feed with companions, a team of otter herding fish into a cove or shallow area, providing food enough for everyone and allowing more time in which to caper.

Yet, when I think of otters, *risk* also comes to mind, perhaps because of the rocks I can see at the slide bottom, knowing that one wrong turn could make the impact quite painful. I wonder where the otters went when rotenone was poured into the river, or when sewage was particularly thick out of nearby homes and mills. I wonder about the dangers they can't smell or see. Fish is their main source of food, and the bigger the fish, the better. But given the recent warnings about what those fish ingest, the bigger the otter's fish, presumably the more it is at risk.

State and federal boards of health have made sure a list of caveats appear in shops where bait and tackle are sold, on sheltered bulletin boards near marinas and launch sites, in the handouts that accompany the purchase of a fishing license. Fish may contain mercury, the materials say, and should not be eaten by pregnant women, or by women who may become pregnant, or by nursing mothers or children under twelve.

A naturally occurring element, mercury exists in sediments and rocks, in oil and coal, and only becomes lethal when it's allowed to accumulate, as can happen when valleys are dammed and waters are slowed, when it seeps out of the sediment and bonds with methane, producing highly toxic methylmercury. Methylmercury causes birth defects, the most graphic examples of which (at least in the photos I saw as a child) are the deformed children of Minamata, Japan, born to parents who ate fish contaminated in the local bay.

A similar risk threatens the Cree, subsistence hunters and fish-eaters in northern Quebec, now that Hydro-Québec, the mega-project supplying electricity to much of the Northeast, has created great lakes out of land that the Cree have long occupied. In the years since the flooding, the native peoples have been warned against eating predatory fish from the lakes (pike, in particular, were said to "make better thermometers than food"). Whitefish, a tribe staple, is risky to eat even at the recommended limit of twice a week. For many local people, who sustained their lives on fish, such a guideline is tough to follow, and their bodies now contain the highest levels of methylmercury of any of Canada's native peoples. Substituting Spam for whitefish proved to be a rotten option.

Another form of mercury, thimerosal, is also often in the news; it's found in the vaccines given to children and frequently raises the question about a possible link to autism (the CDC claims there is no connection, but they have also recommended discontinuing its use). Yet while agencies and parents debate the pros and cons of vaccines, it's not clear who's looking out for otters or for any of the other fish-eating predators in this river— mink, herons, kingfishers, the occasional osprey or eagle. They can't taste the way mercury accumulates; they can't know that large fish contain more than small fish, that each step up the food chain further concentrates the doses.

For an animal that depends on agility for both eating and play, mercury could be the fatal stiffener, a sudden catch in its coordination, the thing that renders it clumsy or stupid. An otter, doing what its body is designed to do, eats one fish too many and crosses that invisible threshold, like a Japanese diner who dares to eat fugu, and the bite he takes is the one that proves fatal.

There is no way to warn otters off their favorite food, yet it would be a diminished place if humans were the only ones finding pleasure on the water. Here is where our emotional worlds overlap, and in the joy that comes with speed and the pleasure of cool water. Though the slide is short, the story is long, written in the smell of dark mud and the imprint of narrow body, relishing the brief and fast run.

5. Town Meeting

The month of May marks the start of town meetings, taking place one by one in small communities across the commonwealth. In Hawley, where the moderator is deaf, the town's business can be completed in about twenty minutes. In Conway, it can take two days. In Leyden, the meetings may go on for six or eight hours, the debates fractious and personal ever since the Board of Health decided to fine a summer resident for his non-permitted outhouse, setting outraged independents against letter-of-the-law public officials. The citizens of Wendell—academics, poets, and back-to-the-land philosophers—may talk for three successive evenings. In Bernardston, where town employees are filing criminal charges against each other, half of them resigning and several others the target of recall petitions, only a few show up for the annual event. The rest have to look elsewhere to restore belief

in a system made up of people doing the best they can to
attend to the needs of their residents.

In Buckland, it's not clear who we are when first
we assemble or what it is we might share, other than a
long stretch of river, a few buildings with public offices,
and a night sky full of stars and little light interference.
Also, pitted roads, much debt, a historic town hall, and
a police force that wants better laws governing foot
traffic on sidewalks.

In the past, lines have been drawn at town gather-
ings between newcomer and old-timer, landowner and
renter, and farmer and commuter, though all of us have
similar reasons for attending. We show up because we
care about this valley and the ways we inhabit it; we care
about kids and schools and taxes and each other. And
tonight we number more than one hundred, gathered in
the high school's auditorium.

In front of us sit the Select Board, the town clerk,
and the town administrator, who helps provide context
for articles on the warrant, along with the Finance Committee, which crafted a $3.25 million budget and which
receives no compensation for its complicated labors. The
moderator, an elected official who receives $250 a year,
stands to one side. Two microphones have been placed at
the end of each aisle.

We shuffle papers—the warrant, the town report,
the budget, the list of classes cut under the school committee's knife—and then begin the evening with the
town report dedication, this year to a man who died
too young, of cancer, who was the town's tree warden
and gypsy-moth superintendent, as well as husband,
father, Little League coach, someone "generous even in
death"—the town administrator chokes up, then manages

to keep reading—when he donated his organs to keep others alive.

Then we launch into the first two articles, formalities each, a warm-up for the work to come, a way to practice making motions and seconding them, and then parsing the words of the committees as they weigh in with recommendations. It takes a few minutes, but soon we're remembering how to do it, how to ask Mr. Moderator for permission to speak before leaping up with a question or comment, how to be good citizens in moving the process forward.

When we reach Article 3, about funding the salaries for elected officials, an impatient voter can't wait any longer. No other expense can be authorized, he insists, until we decide whether we can fund the schools without raising our taxes, something he'll be damned if he will let happen. He moves that we jump to Article 5, and the chair of the finance committee lunges for the microphone. "You care more about your taxes," she rails, "than you do our children!" She can't stop herself; she has invested hours and hours of time in this job and rarely ever gets thanked; she can't let anyone think for a minute that we can't fund education; and of course our children have to take precedence.

The tension is palpable. We can't bail on our schools, which have already lost every single shop and business and home economics class, and most of the art and all of the music. Some study halls go on for eighty minutes, and some classes have more than thirty students assigned to them. Yet to save them means we will have to raise our taxes.

It's also clear that everyone is feeling the pinch of these times. This part of the state fell early into recession; our roads are bad, one of our town's vehicles couldn't pass inspection, and everyone knows the town garage should be razed and replaced, but we can't afford to let it go; instead we'll allot it enough money to patch the walls that leak and the section of ceiling that fell.

We stick to the agenda as written, and there's an audible flexing of muscle when we address the school budget. It's too big a number to contemplate, which, in an odd way, seems to bring us closer together. We utilize procedural maneuvers. We call for a vote to circumvent more discussion. We raise our right hands; we make the big commitment. We pass what the schools need to operate, half of all the money the town will spend this year, and enough to raise our taxes.

We labor on, through Article 10, Article 15, Article 20. Three and a half hours later, we get to Article 21, which outlines an amendment to the town's bylaws, requiring residents to clear their sidewalks of snow. Weariness causes a sudden outburst of jokes. The formal language and need for rules has become too much; we forget to get the nod from Mr. Moderator to speak. Too many people can't keep up with the chore! When the plows dump a load of wet snow on the walkway, it turns to concrete when it freezes, and even a young guy with a snowblower can't deal with it! "I'm pushing seventy," says another man, "and there's no way I can keep up."

"I'm just a girl," says a woman, who must be fifty, "and I can't do it either."

Snow stories get traded, and everyone has at least one. The biggest storm—the one that proved the hardest to move afterwards—left sidewalks so hazardous that people walked in the road, even old folks on clumsy legs, who shouldn't have to deal with traffic in the middle of the street. The simple truth, says another woman, is that there's no way our sidewalks can be used in the winter.

It's the only article thus far that has gone down in defeat.

We come at last to Article 28, the only one that's citizen-generated and which asks us to oppose the Patriot Act. It's a tricky moment. In this warm room, with its many moments of consensus, we are individually Democrat and Republican, Independent and Green. We take pride in thinking for ourselves, in figuring out how to live sustainable lives in a relatively isolated rural area. But passing this article means defying our Congress, our attorney general, our president, joining us with the three hundred or so other towns in the country that have taken similar action.

And on our minds: our auditorium is barely three hours by car from the site of the twin towers. We understand justice and retribution. We have known scares— knives, fights, a wrong turn, somebody's body shoved too close, someone's sweat and frightened smell coming at us—and most of us have felt hurt and the immediate desire to avenge it.

We are also a town defined by a river, and as a result are well versed in damage and recovery. One has only to walk the fields after spring freshets to see layers of rich sediment or crushing acres of new gravel; or wander the potholes at the town's southern edge, formed by violent eddies of gravel swirling for years above soft rock; or recall the Salmon Falls Peace Treaty agreed to by tribes that used to fish here, with all parties promising to ensure safe passage within one day's journey of the area.

Several people prepare to speak; soon someone calls the question, and we agree to end the debate. That sets in motion a vote on the article, which passes quite quickly, with our one consistent naysayer raising his hand in opposition. There is a sudden moment of quiet that no one rushes to fill, and then the moderator bangs down his gavel to end the meeting. That's when we realize just what it is we have done, and we break into applause that lasts for several long minutes.

Acknowledgments

IN THEIR SHAPES AND MEANDERS, the personal essay and the long walk have much in common, most notably in their valuing of the journey over the destination. While the essay seeks to replicate thought, and the walk to take in the view, both wander a terrain fueled as much by sensory input as by the ideas and unlikely juxtapositions that come at us when we're in motion. Both practices involve a heightened attention—to the act of thinking in the essay, to finding the new in the familiar while on a walk—and both often take place alone; neither, however, happens in true isolation. While the walk may be as solitary as the crafting of the work, each requires an engagement with others—family, friends, cohorts, colleagues—with whom to share findings, challenge ideas, and keep digressions relevant.

Many people have aided or accompanied me in some way during the crafting of these essays. Of them, I wish especially to thank Marie-Françoise Hatte and Pat Serrentino, for their work with the Deerfield River Watershed Association, educating me and others about watershed dynamics and engaging me in the bird survey for the Wetland Monitoring Project; also Paul Gorecki, with whom I collected water samples for another DRWA project, and who helped me select flies appropriate for fishing the Deerfield. Sue Morse, Diane Gibbons, and Lorene Wapotich offered a women's tracking workshop at the Rowe Camp & Conference Center in Rowe, Massachusetts (the first annual), which helped further my thinking about the ways we find and narrate stories about wild places. Geoff Brock, Peggy Hart, and Lou Weber, at various times and in various states, made the miles more exciting and the ideas more probable, and I thank Peggy as well for being ever ready to launch a kayak into a river.

Helen Wallace's generous gift of her Cataloochee home, and her and Kim Garcia's thoughtful input, helped me put this collection together during our summer writing retreat. Carol Howard and John Brock, colleagues at Warren Wilson College, kept me on track, during regular feedback sessions, when the distractions became almost too many. Margo Flood, editor of *Heartstone* and director of the Environmental Leadership Center at WWC, provided the necessary support for helping shape "Deciphering *Bird*," and Janisse Ray and Jane Brox, writers in residence during different semesters at the college, offered as much through their insights as through the freedom they gave me to be a student for a short while. It was heartbreaking to lose Kit Ward, who believed in this collection and found it a home with Beacon Press; her premature death left many writers bereft of their champion. Fortunately, Alexis Rizzuto took it under wing and turned the editing process into an engaging and fruitful conversation, and I thank her for such energy and care. To Melissa Dobson, who is extraordinarily keen-eyed about such things as elevations and Blue-Winged Olives: much gratitude for your care in handling these sentences.

Michelle, Katharine, Susan, Gail: thanks for your companionship when we joined together in getting hitched. And Chandra and Rudy: thanks for all you have added to my life over the years—moments tender and awkward and necessary and hard.

I also offer sincere appreciation to my mother for a practice she set in motion when we kids were young and coming home at day's end from various places and adventures. "What did you see today?" she would ask when we had all gathered around the dinner table. "What did you learn?" It became a habit to consider the answers.

Finally, though I pose a tough question in the heart of these essays—What does one do when she loves a person and a place in equal measure?—my love for Holly has helped sustain me in more ways than I can name, and for that I continue to be most grateful.

Notes

HITCHED, MASSACHUSETTS, 2004

"like a really good employee benefits plan . . ." David Brooks, "The Power Of Marriage," *New York Times*, November 22, 2003.
"There are few cynics . . ." Ellen Goodman, "Showing Us the Power of Marriage," *Boston Globe*, May 19, 2004.

HOW TO BECOME A GENERALIST

"like to saw wood . . ." Margaret Fuller, *Woman in the Nineteenth Century* (orig. published New York: Greeley & McElrath, 1845), 160.

COMPANIONS

"Oh what savagery! . . ." Edwin Way Teale, ed., *The Insect World of J. Henri Fabre* (New York: Harpers, 1981), 153.

INTERVENTIONS

"thief, wretch, feathered rat . . . injurious, pernicious, disreputable . . ." Edward Howe Forbush, *Birds of Massachusetts and Other New England States* (Massachusetts Department of Agriculture, 1929). See also Forbush, *Useful Birds and Their Protection* (Massachusetts State Board of Agriculture, 1907).
"Bird feeding is killing birds . . ." Eirik A. T. Blom, "The Problems with Bird Feeding," *Bird Watcher's Digest* 22, no. 1 (September–October 1999): 88–95.

THOREAU ALONE WON'T DO

For Maria Sibylla Merian (1647–1717): see Sharon D. Valiant, "Questioning the Caterpillar: German Naturalist and Artist Maria

Sibylla Merian," *Natural History* 101 (December 1992), and Kim Todd, *Chrysalis: Maria Sibylla Merian and the Secrets of Metamorphosis* (Orlando, FL: Harcourt, 2007). In addition, the National Museum of Women in the Arts, in Washington, DC, has a large number of her prints.
For Cordelia Johnson Stanwood (1865–1958): Chandler S. Richmond, *Beyond the Spring: Cordelia Stanwood of Birdsacre* (Lamoine, ME: Latona Press, 1978). Also: www.birdsacre.com.
For Annie Smith Peck (1850–1935): Elizabeth Fagg Olds, *Women of the Four Winds* [Annie Peck, Delia Akeley, Marguerite Hanson, Louise Boyd] (Boston: Houghton Mifflin, 1985).

AFTER A SWEET SINGING FALL DOWN

the chimney swift "may be less aware of the earth . . ." Rachel Carson, "Ace of Nature's Aviators," in *Lost Woods: The Rediscovered Writing of Rachel Carson*, ed. Linda Lear (Boston: Beacon Press, 1999).
"They show little or no fear" . . . Arthur Cleveland Bent, *Life Histories of North American Cuckoos, Goatsuckers, Hummingbirds and Their Allies, Part II* (New York: Dover, 1964).
"even eminent naturalists of the past generation . . ." Rachel Carson, U.S. Fish & Wildlife Service Press Release, November 12, 1944.
"If reputable persons have not lied to me . . ." Robert MacLeod quoted, along with accounts of Walton and Bartram, in W. L. McAtee, "Torpidity in Birds," *American Midland Naturalist* 38, no. 1 (July 1947). Gilbert White suggests the presence of a nearby *hybernaculum* in *The Natural History and Antiquities of Selborne* (1789).
"For five months [the swift] vanishes . . ." "U.S. Studies Bird Migration; 500,000 Facts, Many Hitherto Unknown, Are Collected by Federal Officials on Flights of Feathered Myriads," *New York Times*, June 20, 1915.
"ornithological fame . . ." Rachel Carson, U.S. Fish & Wildlife Service press release, November 12, 1944.
"The more astonishing, the more true . . ." Andrea Barrett, "Rare Bird," in *Ship Fever: Stories* (New York: Norton, 1996).
the account of two men digging . . . Samuel Williams, *The Natural and Civil History of Vermont* (Walpole, NH, privately printed, 1794).
"and so after a sweet singing fall down . . ." Olaus Magnus, quoted in Elsa Guerdrum Allen, "The History of American Ornithology before Audubon," *Transactions of the American Philosophical Society*, n.s. 41, no. 3 (1951).
For Edmund Jaeger's work on poorwills: www.jaeger.ws/poorwill/index.html.

For Mark Brigham's research on poorwills in British Columbia: "Fun without the Sun in the Okanagan: Unravelling Some of the Mysteries about Bats and Goatsuckers," *Living Landscapes*, Royal BC Museum, http://142.36.5.21/thomp-ok/goatsucker/goatsuckers.htm.

For the veery's song, see David Rothenberg's *Why Birds Sing: A Journey into the Mystery of Bird Song* (New York: Basic Books, 2005); a slowed-down version of its song can be heard at Rothenberg's website, www.whybirdssing.com.

Claims about hibernating birds are still handled cautiously, and the definition of "hibernation" is still in flux. See, for example, Elke Schleucher, "Torpor in Birds: Taxonomy, Energetics, and Ecology," *Physiological and Biochemical Zoology* 77, no. 6 (November/December 2004). "Recent reports on patterns and occurrence of torpor and other natural hypothermic states in birds have prompted a revision of many longstanding opinions."

WILD GEESE AND OTHER NOSTALGIAS

"Coming after the long cold winter . . ." and other quotes from Forbush from Edward Howe Forbush, *Birds of Massachusetts and Other New England States* (Massachusetts Department of Agriculture, 1929).

Though current estimates vary widely . . . "Today, nationwide, there are roughly two-thirds as many resident geese as migrants. In the Atlantic Flyway, the 1.2 million residents actually outnumber migrants by 50 percent." Jack Hope, "The Geese That Came in from the Wild," *Audubon*, March–April 2000, http://archive.audubonmagazine.org/birds/birds0003.html.

"everything is all right, say the meter and the rhyme . . ." Mary Oliver, "A Man Named Frost," in *Winter Hours: Prose, Prose Poems, and Poems* (Boston: Houghton Mifflin, 1999).

RESILIENCE

3. Rotenone

"[I]t may be said that sewage is discharged promiscuously . . ." WPA State Planning Projects, United States Work Progress Administration, *Report on Sources of Pollution, Deerfield River Valley, Massachusetts*, Boston, 1937.

"The best model we have ever had for this disease . . ." Sandra Blakeslee, "Pesticide Found to Produce Parkinson's Symptoms in Rats," *New York Times*, November 5, 2000.

the state wildlife agency poured rotenone into the Deerfield . . . Jim
Mullan and Bill Tompkins, "The Deerfield River Reclamation,"
Massachusetts Wildlife 10, no. 4 (July–August 1959): 3–6. Also:
"The Deerfield River Reclamation" (photo essay), *Massachusetts
Wildlife* 10, no. 6 (November/December 1959).

4. The Slide

"make better thermometers than food" . . . Ted Levin, *Blood Brook: A
Naturalist's Home Ground* (Post Mills, VT: Chelsea Green, 1992).

*the highest levels of methylmercury of any of Canada's native peo-
ples* . . . See *Wikipedia*'s "James Bay Project": http://en.wikipedia
.org/wiki/James_Bay_Project.

vaccines given to children . . . Andrea Rock, "Toxic Tipping Point,"
Mother Jones, March/April 2004.

Printed in the United States
By Bookmasters